D0532539

Library of

Woodbrooke College
Selly Oak
Birmingham

LANCELOT ANDREWES

LANCELOT ANDREWES

by

FLORENCE HIGHAM

SCM PRESS LTD
56 Bloomsbury St., London WC1

274·2

First published January 1952

Printed in Great Britain by
Northumberland Press Limited
Gateshead on Tyne

CONTENTS

CONTENTS

FOREWORD

LANCELOT ANDREWES, who died Bishop of Winchester and left behind him the reputation of a saint and a book of devotions, 'watered with his penitential tears', was born in 1555 in the unhappy reign of Queen Mary. It was in the very months that Mrs. Andrewes, the wife of a master-mariner, awaited the birth of her eldest son in the parish of All Hallows, Barking, that the Queen also waited, at Hampton Court, hoping with a bitter hope that slowly died, that she, like other women, was pregnant and would bear a son. When the symptoms proved false and King Philip sailed away, glad to be rid of an ageing wife and the implacable dislike of her English subjects, the Queen returned to her religion for what comfort she could find and persevered with a ruthlessness, absent from her earlier years, in her attempt to extirpate heresy in England. When she died, many of those she had driven into exile returned to England armed with a Calvinist theology and a militant Protestantism that brought a new tension into the religious situation. The compromise that Elizabeth established by Act of Parliament pleased neither these returned zealots nor the men of the old faith. Only with the passing of time did a new generation, born in the mid-century, grow to maturity, nurtured on the Book of Common Prayer and treading the middle way by choice, not of political necessity. These were the men among whom were numbered Shakespeare and Francis Bacon, Richard Hooker and Lancelot Andrewes. Andrewes died in 1626, in the second year of King Charles' reign when the attack upon the favourite Buckingham fore-shadowed the civil strife that lay ahead. In that conflict the King perished, and the conception of kingship which he had

7

inherited from Elizabeth and James I perished with him; but that other heritage, the Anglican Church, survived, for the Elizabethan compromise enriched and sanctified by faithful lives and the fellowship of worship had proved itself a spiritual reality.

Lancelot Andrewes was one of those who under God helped to bring this spiritual enrichment into the Elizabethan *via media*. It is little enough that we know of this man whose life covered seventy years of such vital import to the English Church. As a person he remains a shadowy figure, pre-eminently a teacher, less easily apprehended than the martyr or the pioneer. As Bishop he shared in James I's failure to comprehend the spiritual vitality of the Puritans and to prevent the tragic cleavage which ensued. Yet the Church he loved so well owed him much. He devoted his wide learning to establishing its claim to be a true part of the great Catholic Church of all ages and did more than any man, save Richard Hooker, to give to the Church of England those particular qualities of sober piety and ordered loveliness in which it has always gloried. By his preaching and still more by his example, as he went humbly but vigorously about his duties, a practical man who never forgot that here he had no continuing city, a saint who knew himself to be a sinner, he showed to the people of his time a pattern of Christian living of which posterity can only catch a glimpse. In the London of Elizabeth's day and later at the court of James I, he stood in the forefront of those who, in a changing world of secular learning and commercial expansion, held firm to eternal values, upheld tradition without losing touch with the world about them, and achieved goodness through no sudden change of heart but by a disciplined life of prayer and worship and complete faith in the promises of God as revealed in the pages of the Scriptures.

I

LONDON AND CAMBRIDGE
1555–88

W H E N he said his prayers and thanked God for all His bless-
ings, Bishop Andrewes, who was never vague either in the
affairs of this world or the next, listed his assets in life and
placed at their head the fact that he was of honest parentage,
and not 'a sorry egg of a sorry crow'. Of his parents we know
nothing except that they came originally from Suffolk and that
his father was a member of Trinity House. Their friendship
with their neighbour Francis Walsingham, who later became
Elizabeth's Principal Secretary, perhaps gives some indication
of their standing. Whether his mother's choice of a name for
her first-born is the sign of a romantic temperament, one cannot tell. Fifty years later she might have christened him Josiah
or Ebenezer, but the Bible in English was still a rare possession
in 1555, and every chapman, calling his ballads down the
London streets, would have among his stock-in-trade tales of
the Round Table. As he grew out of babyhood, she found
him indeed a son to be proud of, gifted beyond his peers in
matters of schooling, yet healthy in body and eager in mind.
At a tender age he was sent to the Cooper's Free School at
Ratcliffe. It was his father's intention to apprentice him to a
trade, but both Walsingham and Dr. Ward the headmaster
dissuaded him, discerning a potential scholar in the quick-
witted and industrious little boy, and in 1561, when he was six,
Lancelot was offered a place, among a hundred poor scholars,
in the new school founded by the Merchant-Taylors Company.

How many of the great men of the sixteenth and seventeenth century owed their chance in life to the local grammar school! There was no segregation of classes in the education of the young in Elizabeth's day, and where there were brains there was opportunity. Dean Colet's foundation at St. Paul's in 1512 and Christ's Hospital set up on the site of the dissolved Greyfriars in 1533 take pride of place among the London schools but, as England's prosperity increased, the Guilds and Trading Corporations followed the example of individuals and in 1561 the Merchant-Taylors founded what Stowe describes as ' a notable free Grammar School '.

Not far from Lower Thames Street where Andrewes lived, in the parish of St. Laurence Pulteney, there was an old house known as the Manor of the Rose, which the Merchant-Taylors purchased, and here young Andrewes went to school, beginning lessons at seven o'clock, no early hour for him who was already in the habit of getting up at 4 a.m. to study. The first headmaster, Mr. Richard Mulcaster, was something of an eccentric and Fuller in his Church History relates that ' he would exactly and plainly construe and parse the lesson to his scholars, which done, he slept his hour (custom made him critical to proportion it) in his desk in the school, but woe be to the scholar that slept awhile! ' He was of a choleric temper, and his tenure of office was marked by numerous quarrels with his governors. They complained for one thing that he would not be polite to school visitors and he gave short shrift to parents. ' The prayers of cockering mothers prevailed with him as much as the requests of indulgent fathers, rather increasing than mitigating his severity on their offending children.'

Lancelot Andrewes was a pupil after his own heart. Mulcaster's own speciality was Oriental languages, and Hebrew was taught in the school. Andrewes' genius was of the painstaking type, and in an age of infant prodigies he was not outstandingly brilliant or original in his thought. But Mulcaster discovered in him an aptitude for languages as great as his own. He had a prodigious memory, and his nimble wit and unruffled good humour made him a delight to teach. He had the enquiring temper and the mental integrity which are the marks of a true scholar and which in a later century might have combined with his interest in external phenomena to make him a great scientist; born into the age of the Renaissance and Reformation he took as naturally as a duck to water to the study of ancient tongues, with the Greek philosophers and the Holy Scriptures as the glorious text books with which each day he grew more familiar. There was no going into day-dreams for him, as no doubt happened with his younger school-mate Edmund Spenser. A passage from Virgil, or a psalm in the Hebrew original, might send the young Spenser chasing images down the paths of fancy. But Andrewes was far too fascinated by the structure of languages to let his attention wander. Under Mulcaster's inspiring guidance, he learnt not only Greek and Latin and Hebrew but the interplay of sound and sense, the discipline of grammar and the increasing interest of analysing and comparing foreign tongues.

One does not know what part he took in the school plays, performed each year before the Court, whereby the headmaster hoped to teach his self-assertive or tongue-tied boys 'audacity and good behaviour' according to their need. It may be that thus he first acquired those tricks of dramatic gesture and voice control which added so much in later years to his effectiveness as a preacher.

In 1571, Andrewes went up to Cambridge. A school-fellow described him to Aubrey as 'a great long boy' at the time and he must have had something of a reputation, for that autumn he had the opportunity to go to either university. His name appears in the records of Jesus College, Oxford, as one of the foundation scholars appointed by the Queen. But Dr. Watts, a Prebendary of St. Paul's and Archdeacon of Middlesex, had recently given two farms to Pembroke Hall 'for the maintenance of seven scholars long known by the glorious name of Greek scholars'. Four of these scholarships were offered to boys from Merchant-Taylors school, and first among those elected was Lancelot Andrewes.

Andrewes spent more than fifteen years of his life at Cambridge, at first as student, later as don. He graduated in 1575 and received a Fellowship next year, after a competitive examination with Thomas Dove, another old Merchant-Taylors boy. He was ordained deacon in 1580 and priest in 1581. It was not till 1586, after his appointment as chaplain to the Archbishop of Canterbury, that he emerged into a wider sphere of influence; and a new chapter opened two or three years later when he received the care of a city church and came to reside in London. His career at Cambridge was crowned by the Mastership of his college in 1589.

So much for the facts; it is less easy to estimate the effect upon his character of the fifteen years he spent in residence at Pembroke Hall. The strenuous life of a student, the friendly rivalry with Dove, his growing reputation both for scholarship and piety, and the pleasure he derived from the beauty of Cambridge and the friendships of university life, all played their part in moulding Lancelot Andrewes. We can imagine that he lived an ordered, disciplined life, for by such habits his natural disposition was strengthened and confirmed, and they were maintained to the end of his days. Even when he entered public life, he liked to remain until midday in the privacy of his study and was as near to irritation as he could be when friends disturbed him then, whereas in the afternoon he was ready and willing to immerse himself in any business on hand, his own, or other people's. He had few relaxations, but walking he did enjoy and in the vacation it was his custom to make the journey to London on foot, but it was characteristic of him that he stopped walking home when someone pointed out to him that it looked as if he could not afford a conveyance; there was a streak of conventionality in him that forbade any incursion into eccentricity. Allied to this was the painstaking attention to detail which characterized alike his scholarship, his dress and his conduct of practical affairs. If it had not been for his eager response to the beauty of the world about him, and for the genuine kindness with which he regarded his fellow men, he might not have stood out among the many scholars of eminence that the university boasted. As it was, he must have been, as the years advanced, a well-known and well-loved figure in the streets of Cambridge, for his conversation was salted with a cockney humour, his temper was always serene, and he had never been known wittingly to hurt a soul.

These to a large extent were gifts of nature, the gentle flowering in the sun of a temperament exactly suited to the life of a university don. But there were signs, too, of gifts of grace. Many of those hours that Andrewes spent in the privacy of his rooms were spent at prayer and, though the work of the Holy Spirit would only become manifest when the sufferings and frustrations of maturity had laid their mark upon him, he bore, even in his young manhood, the signs of a dedicated life.

After he became a Fellow, Andrewes devoted himself to acquiring a new language every year, arranging beforehand with his parents to engage him a tutor for the month he spent in London. According to Fuller, he became ' so skilled in all, especially Oriental languages, that some conceive he might (if then living) almost have served as an interpreter-general at the confusion of tongues'. He was also engaged on those Patristic studies which he was to make his own particular field of enquiry. And as his interest in theology grew, a new opportunity of service developed which revealed in him unexpected gifts. His appointment as Catechist to the College after his ordination gave him scope as a teacher and as a preacher and in both spheres he was a remarkable success. His clarity of thought, his powers of analysis and his sympathetic approach to the difficulties, moral and intellectual, of his hearers made him not only an excellent exponent of moral theology but a true shepherd of souls.

As catechist, he instituted a course of week-end lectures on the Decalogue, to which town and gown came in growing numbers. There was something in the manner of Andrewes' delivery that time has blotted out for us, that went straight to the hearts of the hearers. By an intellectual assault upon the matter in hand that wrested every ounce of meaning out of word and phrase, he carried his audience triumphantly in his wake, and he crowned his argument by a simple, unanswerable spiritual appeal. If at the end there were individuals still at a loss, the Don came down from the rostrum and was ready with common sense and kindliness to give the comfort and advice required. One stout Alderman, for example, found that he always fell asleep when he listened to a sermon on Sunday afternoon. He consulted Andrewes who advised him not to eat so large a midday meal. The Alderman complied, but alas! he still fell asleep. He came again for advice, fearful that his soul was in imminent danger. But the practical Andrewes bade him not to despair, but to take his dinner earlier, eat as much as he wished and have a good nap afterwards before he came to church.

Throughout the lectures Andrewes showed a like shrewd sympathy which kept him, despite his learning, closely in touch with the ordinary man. He introduced his pupils gently to the Bible, for he declared 'in some places of the scripture the lamb may wade, so in others the elephant may swim'. He extolled the need for faith but urged none to despair 'for though faith be a perfect way, we walk unperfectly in it'. 'We must look to God for His spirit and inspiration', and by reliance on prayer and not despising the use of reason 'grow to perfection little by little'. 'He that believeth,' he added, 'shall not make haste.' This conception of the Christian life as one of gradual growth into the full stature of the sons of God, was as typical of him as his determination in his lectures to steer clear of all tendentious matter, basing his teaching on the fundamental doctrines of the Church. The incarnation, the atonement, the resurrection, the full Gospel of Christ, bearing with it the two-fold obligation to glorify God and love the brethren, here man could find all he needed to keep him from falling and to lead him into everlasting life.

The years that Lancelot Andrewes spent at Cambridge were years of comparative calm in an era of theological strife. In its beginning, the Reformation had been largely a matter of politics, but the translation of the Scriptures into the vernacular gave every literate man a chance to think out his faith for himself, and with new ideas stirring in a thousand heads a return to former ways could scarcely be imagined. The brief reign of Edward VI bequeathed to the reformed Church a liturgy of unsurpassed loveliness, and Mary's hapless persecutions gave it its first martyrs. Elizabeth compromised, dropping the offending title of Head of the Church only to assume that of Governor, and in the administration of Holy Communion striving to reconcile conflicting beliefs by including sentences expressive of both. The Pope's authority had gone for good, but discipline and all that the idea of authority implied was an integral part of any contemporary conception of the Church, and the Crown stepped firmly into the place of the Papacy. There was nothing incongruous in this in an age of growing national consciousness and Elizabeth hoped, by lack of explicitness on matters of dogma, to make possible the loyal adherence of all law-abiding Englishmen. Two sets of circumstances prevented her success, Mary Stuart's presence in England after 1568, a rallying point for discontented Roman Catholics, and at the other extreme the advanced opinions of the Protestant exiles who had returned from Geneva and elsewhere upon Elizabeth's accession. The undergraduates at Cambridge in 1564, who showed their abhorrence of Catholic practices by flinging a dead dog at the elevated Host, disgusted sober men, always in dread of excesses comparable to those of the German anabaptists. But none the less the majority of the godly and learned in both universities desired something much more far-reaching than Elizabeth's immediate compromise and expected it, as times grew more settled, to advance to a more ruthless extermination of Papist practices, to a more clearly defined theology and to some modification of episcopal government. For the greater part of the reign, it remained an open question whether or not men of this type could be persuaded to give their devoted adherence to the Elizabethan settlement, thus breathing into the bare bones of a political compromise the life and warmth of a spiritual reality. Could they fit themselves into an authoritarian Church and reconcile their consciences with the dictates of a Tudor sovereign? Or had that been set in motion which could not now be checked, a drift away from authority and the idea of community, towards separatism, antinomianism and the like?

The decade before Andrewes' arrival at Cambridge had been thick with controversy. Certain 'irritable precisians', as Archbishop Parker called them, objected to the wearing of vestments, and the outspoken preaching of Thomas Cartwright, Fellow of Trinity and Lady Margaret Professor, revealed a chasm that could not easily be bridged between the Church as they envisaged it and Elizabeth's *via media*. They suspected authority in a way sufficient in itself to secure the Queen's disapprobation. She was not likely to overlook a casual remark of Cartwright's that 'it was not absolutely necessary that there should be one over all in a Commonwealth', and in 1570 Cartwright was silenced by Whitgift, the Master of Trinity, who ejected him from his Chair, and two years later, with much less justification, deprived him of his Fellowship.

Andrewes' first years as an undergraduate were spent in a Cambridge turbulent and yet weary of turbulence. The disorder was checked by certain administrative reforms, and gradually a real revival set in. The point of view for which Cartwright had stood continued to have its champions, and the foundation of Emmanuel College in 1584 provided the Puritans of the next generation with their intellectual headquarters.

The piety and learning of many of the precisians made it unthinkable that they should not play their part in moulding the Elizabethan settlement, the more so as there was as yet no clear doctrinal divergence. To a young man of Andrewes' temper, the group that had developed under Cartwright's leadership appeared by far the most congenial in the university, and when he became a Fellow he often associated with them. According to one story he was only dissuaded from a closer alliance by a friendly stratagem. One, who wished to open his eyes to the danger of extremes, took him first to hear a sermon inveighing against sport on the Sabbath day and then showed him a private door opening on to the bowling green of the preacher's college. There, with their gowns and their principles laid aside, the preacher and his friends were enjoying a game of bowls.

The story no doubt is apocryphal but the fact remains of Andrewes' gradual alienation from the Puritans. As with every year he was steeped more thoroughly in the story of the early Church and the lives and teaching of the Christian Fathers, it was the feeling of continuity that he prized most highly, and he could not divorce from his religious experience all the beauty of worship, the richness of philosophic thought and the examples of saintly living that were part of the heritage of medieval Christendom. He clung to the fact that the Elizabethan Church, reformed though it was, remained in all essentials Catholic. But he was very English—it is a curious fact that this scholar of a European reputation, this man of many tongues, never went abroad. Thanks to his learning he was never insular, but his whole background and his full share of the exuberant national spirit of his age made him a ready champion of an English Church, that gave to the Crown rather than the Papacy supreme authority in matters ecclesiastical. And it was on this wing that the struggle raged in the country at large during the years that Andrewes was at Cambridge. The full force of the Counter-Reformation was directed upon England. As early as 1572, on his first Long Vacation, Andrewes must have found his people at home even more disturbed than other London households by the calamitous news of the massacre of St. Bartholomew. For their friend Francis Walsingham was himself in Paris, as secretary to the English Ambassador, and had seen and experienced the horrors of the night. Next year, Walsingham became one of the Queen's Principal Secretaries and wore himself out in her service, defending her from the danger of attack which increased considerably after the Pope had issued his Bill of deposition. During the next few years the tension steadily grew. From the new seminaries which Catholic piety had founded overseas for the education of their sons, a constant stream of Jesuit missionaries poured into England to give their lives for their faith. Their aims were spiritual but, once in the government's hands, their refusal to take the oath of supremacy made it possible to execute them as traitors and the emergency seemed to justify severity. In 1583 Whitgift was called from Cambridge to succeed the lenient Grindal in the Primacy.

Small and dark, able and adamant, a disciplinarian by instinct and full of mental and physical energy, Whitgift was dubbed by Elizabeth 'her little black husband', and though his lack of caution often angered her, she entrusted him in the main with the care of the Church in these difficult years of crises. The discovery of the Throgmorton conspiracy and of a perfectly feasible plan to invade England and to assassinate the Queen brought everyone, except the Queen herself, to the verge of panic. Five priests, who had nothing to do with the plot, were hung at Tyburn, and the prisons were full of recusants. Fortunately the Queen's fortitude and the nation's common sense prevented the panic from spreading, although the murder of William of Orange in the June of '84 brought the danger of assassination very close. It was all the more credit to Whitgift and Burghley that at this stage they decided to try reason as well as force. The Archbishop knew of none more likely to convince one large group of prisoners at Wisbeach Castle, a regular place of captivity for recusants, than his chaplain, Lancelot Andrewes, who was therefore summoned from the shelter of the university to play his part in the controversies of the time.

What success he had with the recusants we do not know. That he treated them with respect and kindliness we may be certain. Years afterwards when, as Bishop of Ely, he had charge of the castle at Wisbeach with its complement of captives, he did his utmost to ameliorate their condition, saying that he would not add affliction to the afflicted. It must have been with relief that he returned for a short time to Cambridge. But it was not for long.

Others beside Whitgift had him in mind. Walsingham was at the very centre of a knot of influential noblemen, who hoped for various ends to drive the Queen further along the the path of ultra-Protestantism. Leicester was their leader at court and his nephew, Philip Sidney, was married to Walsingham's daughter. After Orange's murder the Queen reluctantly allowed Leicester to captain a small expeditionary force which resulted only in the battle of Zutphen and the death of Philip Sidney. In 1586, the year that Zutphen was fought, Andrewes accompanied the Earl of Huntingdon, President of the Council of the North, on a tour of the northern counties. As chaplain to the Earl, a man of Puritan tendencies, he was again mainly concerned in debates with Roman Catholics, and it was natural that Secretary Walsingham should wonder if further use might not be made of him. He summoned him from Cambridge to a private interview, and thereupon urged him, if given preferment, to uphold in public the advanced form of Protestantism for which Walsingham and his colleagues stood. But according to Sir John Harington, the Queen's godson, who records this interview, Andrewes showed himself unexpectedly adamant. He was not one ' to be scared with a Councillor's frown or blown aside with his breath ', and he answered Walsingham plainly that such a championship of the Puritan viewpoint would be ' not only against his learning but his conscience '. But, Harington continues, ' The Councillor seeing this man would be no Friar Pinkie (to be taught in a closet what he should say at Pauls) dismissed him with some disdain at the time; but afterwards did the more reverence his integrity and honesty and became no hindrance to his ensuing preferments '.

In the next few years those ' ensuing preferments ' came thick and fast. In 1588 or early next year, he received the benefice of St. Giles, Cripplegate, and in 1589 was appointed to a Prebendal stall at Southwell and a residential canonry at St. Paul's. He said good-bye to the university and came to live in London, but his connection with Cambridge was maintained by his appointment as Master of Pembroke, and so far was he from regarding this as a sinecure that in his years of office he succeeded in transforming the deficit with which he began into a healthy balance of £1,000. His interest in the college was always maintained, and he often interviewed scholarship candidates, sometimes very characteristically paying the fees of the unsuccessful competitor. His feet were set on the road to riches but one debt would always remain, the debt he owed to Cambridge for years of quiet and uneventful happiness, permeated with the disciplined joy of the scholar's search for truth.

II

LONDON AND WESTMINSTER
1588-1605

LONDON in the year of the Armada; with Sir Thomas Gresham's new Exchange witnessing to its growing prosperity, with its old walls still in being and crowding about them, to the east the Tower, sombre and terrible, to the north the fields, where the trained bands drilled and shot, to the west the Temple and Lincoln's Inn, and southward, the River Thames. What a time and what a city in which to take one's place among those who were moulding England! Since Hugh Latimer had stirred to anger or delight the folk of the mid-century, London had been starved of great preachers. But this year at the Spitalfields, where every Easter sermons were preached by a Bishop, a Dean and a Doctor of Divinity, Dr. Andrewes inveighed against 'high-minded men', scolding them for their unwillingness 'to be pruned and trimmed' by the word of the Almighty, and beseeching them, 'Oh beloved, you that be in wealth and authority, love and reverence the word of God'.

'Talk not of faith,' this new preacher cried on another occasion. 'You have no faith in you; tell me not of your religion for there is no religion in you, pure religion is this, to visit the fatherless and widows.' Thus began thirty-five years of deepening influence, as the quiet, unassuming man who became, it was said, 'an angel in the pulpit', drove home to all sorts and conditions of men the fundamental truths of the Gospel. The bare notes alone are left to us; sufficient to illus-

trate that juxtaposition of erudition and tenderness that gave
the sermons their peculiar character, revealing only dimly the
vigour of attack, the scholar's enjoyment in the meaning of
words, above all the radiance of an integrated Christian personality. One must imagine, if one can, the church of St.
Giles, where they laid Martin Frobisher to rest in 1594, and
where the tailor-historian, Mr. Spede, sat, with his young wife,
under the new Vicar. One must recall the fine Gothic arches
of old St. Paul's and envisage the crowded chapel at Whitehall
on the frequent occasions when he preached before the Queen,
and place the tall but slender figure of Lancelot Andrewes,
with his long, narrow face, his trim beard and his expressive
hands not against the dusty background of eleven volumes in
the library of Anglo-Catholic theology but in the exuberant
setting of Elizabethan London.

Another aspect of his work in London, too, gave Andrewes
peculiar satisfaction. As Canon of St. Paul's, he occupied the
stall which was traditionally that of the Penitentiary, and he
saw no reason why he should not continue the ancient custom
of confession. The 'ghostly counsel' of a trained minister
might direct aright many a darkened spirit, conscious less of
definite sin than of an aching need and a wilderness of doubt.
'This is the triumph of religion, the riotous person, the atheist,
the hypocrite, all shall seek,' he said on one occasion, and to
the end of his life he felt it to be his prime duty to help those
who sought. Here in St. Paul's was the world in microcosm;
in the crowded transept all sorts and conditions of men con-
versed, whispered, or rubbed shoulders with their neighbours
as they cut across the church about their business. But
when the season of Lent came round, they became aware of
a grave figure who walked daily in the south aisle welcoming
any who would speak with him. As in the week-end lectures
at Cambridge, so now in the Cathedral, Andrewes applied his
gift of spiritual healing to the tangled lives of ordinary men
and women, quietly persisting in the face of criticism at the
revival of a 'Popish' practice. Let theologians dispute if they
wished the meaning of Absolution, it sufficed him that he

could bring comfort to the aching hearts and puzzled minds of those who walked and talked in Paul's, and give them a new comprehension of the meaning of divine compassion.

Of Andrewes' private life during the years in London we know extremely little. One of the rare references is to continued contact with the Walsingham family. Sir Francis had died in 1590, worn out in the Queen's service, and about the same time his daughter, Philip Sidney's widow, had been married secretly to the Earl of Essex, the wayward young man who had succeeded Leicester in the ageing Queen's affections. When the secret of the marriage was revealed her anger was intense, and Essex was only restored to favour upon promising that his wife should live 'very retired in her mother's house'. It was there, in January 1591, that Lancelot Andrewes christened privately the son born of the marriage. It was well that the future was hid from the little group of friends who gathered to bid the child 'God-speed', for little of happiness lay in store for the second Earl of Essex.

For Andrewes the London years were mainly occupied in pastoral duties and in a contented bachelordom enriched by friendships with most of the men of culture in a brilliant age. Andrewes never married and one does not know whether he remained a bachelor from principle or chance. But it seemed as if the love he could not expend on wife and child was poured out upon all humanity, and his gentleness was so marked as to be a positive quality, not merely an absence of passion or impatience. But as prominent in his make-up as this serenity was his industry, and his growing influence was at least in part due to his effectiveness. Whether he was dealing with the affairs of his parish, his college accounts, or his varied duties as one of Whitgift's chaplains, he was not only honest and kind, he was hard-working and efficient. He showed himself a true Elizabethan in his sturdy respect for property and in his attention to practical details and to the material well-being of those whose affairs were in his hands. Every piece of work was a task to be done to the glory of God, and since he knew that the cut flower soon withers, he rooted all his work in worship, so that the hours at his desk, in the pulpit or the city street were surrounded and enriched by the hours he spent in prayer.

Prayer, study, the practical duties of his station, and, all too often, controversy! He could not entirely escape it for once again the air was rife with disputes. The execution of Mary Stuart, followed by the defeat of the Armada, had relieved the political tension and the immediate threat from Rome. But the Protestants of the school of Cartwright were still restive and there was a new phenomenon in the appearance of groups who adopted the idea of independent congregations as out-lined by Robert Browne. In their conception of a congrega-tion as a fellowship of dedicated individuals there was much that was noble, but it ran counter to the Catholic ideal of the Church as one organic whole. To these extremists, even more than to Cartwright and his friends, episcopacy was an obvious object of attack, for the continuity and discipline which were so precious to Andrewes proved a stumbling-block to them. In the very year that the Armada was fought, a series of tracts emanating from various secret presses appeared under the pseudonym Martin Marprelate. Not mincing their words, they attacked bishops and their ' garb, gait, apparel, vanities of their youth, natural defects and personal infirmities '. The probable author of these tracts was a Welshman, John Penry, but in 1590 a friend of his, Dr. Udall, was cited before the Court of High Commission as in part responsible. Udall, at one time the respected Vicar of Kingston-on-Thames, was a man of true piety and learning and an advanced Puritan who looked for scriptural authority for all his actions. He refused to admit complicity, but was not allowed counsel and was most unjustly imprisoned and sentenced to death. No attempt was made to execute the sentence and, in the face of growing public opinion, he was eventually reprieved, but before the release was effected he fell ill and died in prison.

During his captivity he was frequently visited by Dr. Andrewes. He could make no headway against Udall's con-victions but there grew up between the two men the mutual respect of Christians. Like so many others Udall found comfort in Andrewes' presence and asked that he might often visit him. Next year, Henry Barrow and his associate Greenwood were seized at a separatist meeting and condemned to death for treason. Once more Andrewes visited the condemned cell, but he and Barrow spoke a different language and it was with a sense of failure and frustration that he went away. The cruel sentence was carried out and yet another rift was made in the fabric of the universal Church.

It was about this time that Andrewes fell seriously ill from worry and overwork. He believed that the essential truths of the gospel were manifest and that little could be gained from theological debate. 'We are ever saying much of the diffusion of the light, nothing of the supplying of the oil,' he cried. He looked around him at those who represented the Church in the world. What could give to the lax clergy and the indifferent congregations something of the zeal and devotion which had moved Campion and Udall alike, but which was sadly to seek in the choir stalls and the high pews of cathedral and village church. The Holy Spirit alone could do it. 'Weak in appearance as It is,' so he declared in one of his sermons, 'by It were great things brought to pass. By this breath of breath was the world blown about.' So it happened again in Elizabethan England. While Essex strode on to power and disaster, while Whitgift tried in vain to sweep back the rising tide of Puritanism and the Commons grew steadily in insolence and power, the judicious Hooker meditated, and in 1594 published the first four volumes of the *Eccesliastical Polity*.

We do not know how intimately Andrewes and Hooker were acquainted. At first their paths running parallel had much in common, for both were scholars, rejoicing in learning for its own sake, never considering compromise with the truth, and in their sympathies and range sharing in the scholastic life of Europe. Each was gentle in temper and grave of bearing, his devotional life, and by degrees his whole being, steeped in the spirit and the cadences of the Book of Common Prayer.

But Hooker had the more masculine intellect; under his shy exterior there was an emotional fire that Andrewes perhaps lacked, and above all he was fortunate—or strong-minded enough—not to become a success at court. So he was able, in retirement, to think out from the beginning the meaning of his faith and how it differed alike from that of Calvin and that of Rome.

In the spring of 1585 Hooker had become Master of the Temple, and it was there he had his first tussle with Puritanism in the person of the polite but obdurate Mr. Travers, who, as afternoon lecturer, contradicted each Sunday the tenets preached by Mr. Hooker in the morning. They were both too good Christians to let personal animosity embitter the dispute, but the altercation made quiet thought impossible and Hooker begged leave to resign, that he might clarify his ideas in the comparative calm of a country parish. His premature death before the turn of the century robbed England of one of her finest intellects at a time when she stood in sore need of the sweet reasonableness and the mental rectitude which characterized Hooker's thought.

When he heard of Hooker's death, Andrewes wrote to a friend: 'I never failed since I last saw you but daily prayed for him till this very instant you sent this heavy news. And whether I shall live to know any near him, I am in great doubt.' In a postcript he warned his correspondent to see that Hooker's manuscripts were taken into safe custody, advice not immediately followed, with the tragic result that the later volumes were either destroyed or mislaid.[1]

The main thesis of the *Ecclesiastical Polity* is the justification of reason as a means whereby faith may be attained and strengthened, and by reason Hooker did not mean man's individual opinions but 'true, sound, divine reason' as exemplified in God's laws and in the gathered wisdom of the ages. There was something very English about Hooker's philosophy; he stood in theology where Shakespeare stood in

---

[1] See C. J. Sisson, *The Judicious Marriage of Mr. Hooker*, pp. 98-107 *et alia*, for an account of the MS and Andrewes' share in preserving part of it.

the realm of English literature, Spenser in pure poesy, and the great Queen herself in politics, and the *Ecclesiastical Polity* is imbued with the English way of thought, with a wide tolerance, a pride in the traditions of the past and a deep respect for law. It contains little metaphysic, but as T. S. Eliot writes in his *Essays on Faith and Order*, to which he gave the name *For Lancelot Andrewes*, 'the intellectual achievement and the prose style of Hooker and Andrewes came to complete the structure of the English Church as the philosophy of the thirteenth century crowns the Catholic Church'. He argues that they made 'the English Church more worthy of intellectual assent' and that their writings illustrated 'that determination to stick to essentials, that awareness of the needs of the time, the desire for clarity and precision on matters of importance, and the indifference to matters indifferent which was the general policy of Elizabeth'.

In 1597 Andrewes declared that since his ordination seventeen years before he had never preached in public or private on such nice points of dogma as predestination. Hooker remained a Calvinist in his theology, but he was at one with Andrewes in the width of his interpretation and in his keen sense of the processes of history so that he urged men in their religious life to draw not only upon the Scriptures and their own resources, but on tradition with all its riches and upon the pronouncements of the Church. He insisted that in matters other than the great fundamentals of doctrine, the authority of the Church should be obeyed; just as in matters of State the Crown was omnicompetent. Hooker struck a new note here, in identifying the Crown with the State and in upholding the Crown and the episcopacy, as incomparably the best instruments whereby harmony in State and Church could be accomplished. This question of authority, so integral a part of the good life as Hooker envisaged it, was one to which in the succeeding years many men were to find diverse answers, till it became the dominating question alike in politics and religion.

In 1595 there was an unfortunate outburst of energy on

Whitgift's part which resulted in the issue from Lambeth of certain articles of faith of a definite Calvinist character. The Archbishop had been annoyed by fresh disturbances at Cambridge, where a certain William Barrett had in his sermons denounced predestination. Whitgift, a Calvinist in matters of doctrine, censured Barrett and issued the articles as a statement of the Church's faith. Many were seriously disquieted, and Andrewes clearly expressed his own distaste for the articles in his 'censure on the censure' of Barrett. 'The cause of man not being drawn to God,' he asserted, 'is the depraved will of man, not the absolute will of God.' And he went on to argue that although good works to be of any avail must be the fruit of 'our incision and engrafting onto Christ' and 'we must wholly depart out of ourselves, we must not conceive that there is any sufficiency in ourselves but that all our sufficiency is of God', yet 'a complete obedience on our part in the use of all the prescribed means never did go away empty from Him or without blessing: never did nor never shall'.

Here were two distinct approaches to the truth. The Calvinist faith in the Sovereignty of God and the doctrine of election gave to the Puritans of the next generation a conviction of righteousness which nerved them to do battle for the Lord. From the ranks of these were to come the men who founded New England, the soldiers who fought in Cromwell's army, the faithful whose courage under persecution gave to England the great heritage of the Free Churches. Apart from the spiritual strength of their witness, there was also much that was of value, as a bulwark against tyranny, in their stress on the importance of the individual. But there was a second way, the way that the Caroline Churchmen were to tread, basing themselves on the teaching of Hooker and Andrewes. To them, the life of a Christian was an earthly pilgrimage to which the worship of the Church brought refreshment and in which the soul might find, in prayer and sacraments and the pages of the Holy Scriptures, the comfort and guidance sufficient for his need. It was with a gentle radiance rather than a sudden effulgence that the light shone about their path, but when the crisis came in the tragedy of the Civil War, these men, too, showed that they could suffer for their faith.

The Lambeth articles were recalled at the Queen's command, and for a while there were no further crises in religious matters. None of the problems had been solved and everything depended on the personality of the sovereign, facts that might well disturb thoughtful men, but most of the dissatisfied, recusant and Puritan alike, looked hopefully towards James Stuart, the heir-presumptive, the king of John Knox's country, the son of a Catholic mother, and hoped that with his coming a more prosperous age would dawn for their section of the community.

Meanwhile Elizabeth would have liked to have seen Andrewes on her bench of bishops. In 1596 he was offered the Bishopric of Salisbury and three years later that of Ely. But the Queen was accustomed to increase her income by keeping the sees vacant and appropriating the revenues, and Andrewes refused promotion as a protest against this habit. Elizabeth bore him no malice; he was preferred to a stall at Westminster in 1598, and in 1601 he became Dean, a position which brought him into close contact with Westminster School, the medieval College of St. Peters which had been refounded by Elizabeth in 1561. And so, unexpectedly, as he approached his fiftieth year, he found himself removed a little way from political tumults and ecclesiastical disputes to live again in the atmosphere of learning and teaching which he loved.

It was a hard regime at Westminster School. From five in the morning till eight at night the boys laboured, the headmaster's birch and the petty tyranny of monitors adding to their burden. Meals were held in common and it was here that Dean Andrewes would customarily meet the boys. No doubt he played his part with equanimity in the Shrovetide 'rag' when the school cook tossed the pancake and any boy who caught it could claim a guinea from the Dean. There were no set holidays, but Andrewes' predecessor had noticed

how the boys wilted during the summer months and had purchased a house in Chiswick where they could have a measure
of ease and recreation and be secure from the Plague which
so often ravaged London in the summer. There was a viru-
lent outbreak in 1603 and Andrewes' presence at Chiswick at
that time has been unjustly criticized, for he was there in
charge of the school, and returned to Westminster before the
epidemic ceased, with some of the senior boys who were pre-
paring for the university.

In 1620, Williams, newly appointed Dean of Westminster,
and anxious to model himself on his great predecessor, cross-
examined his protégé Hacket about Andrewes' régime. In
his life of Bishop Williams, Hacket tells of this interview and
apologizes for the digression with the words, 'For who could
come near to the shrine of such a saint [as Andrewes] and not
offer up a few grains of glory upon it or how dare I omit it?
For he was the first that planted me in my tender studies and
water'd them continually with his Bounty.' He goes on to
describe how Andrewes loved to walk with the boys and to
talk to them, 'he never walked to Chiswick for his recreation
without a brace of this young Fry, and in that way-faring
leisure, had a singular dexterity to fill those narrow vessels with
a Funnel'. The rest of Hacket's report to Williams gives an
equally vivid picture of Andrewes eagerly taking every
opportunity of infecting others with his own zeal for learning.
'I told him,' Hacket writes, 'how strict that excellent man
was, to charge our masters that they should give us lessons
out of none but the most Classical Authors; that he did often
supply the Place both of Head School-Master and Usher for
the Space of an whole week together and gave us not an hour
of Loitering time from morning to night. How he caused
our exercises in prose and verse to be brought to him to examine our Style and Proficiency. And which was the greatest
burden of his Toil, sometimes thrice in a week, sometimes
oftener, he sent for the uppermost Scholars to his Lodgings at
night, and kept them with him from eight till eleven, un-
folding to them the best Rudiments of the Greek Tongue,

and the Elements of the Hebrew Grammar, and all this he did to Boys without any compulsion of Correction; nay I never heard him utter so much as a word of austerity among us.' It was the compulsion of love which Andrewes employed and which enabled him not merely to instruct his hearers but to lead them into a fuller comprehension of all that truth and virtue meant. A generation of scholars, among whom was George Herbert as well as Hacket, never forgot his example or his teaching, 'the ointment of whose name is sweeter than all spices'.

As usual, Andrewes was effective in his stewardship, leaving Westminster 'a place truly exemplarily collegiate in all respects both within and without; free from debts and arrearage, from encroachments and evil customs'. He had in like manner improved the state of St. Giles and had built a house in Creed Lane for the prebendary at St. Paul's. But as his wealth increased, so did his alms, and 'he stayed not till the poor sought him', but used in his charity imagination as well as sympathy. Meanwhile the great school on his doorstep provided him with the warm human relationships which his celibate life must sometimes have lacked, while his pastoral work at St. Giles and his growing influence, through his sermons, at Whitehall gave him the satisfaction of Christian witness and fellowship. But time was not standing still, and across these happy years there fell, in the spring of 1603, a dark shadow, a long-expected calamity. Queen Elizabeth died. It was Andrewes who preached the funeral sermon when the great queen was buried in the Abbey. As he bade farewell to his royal mistress and mourned the passing of a great age, he could not know that his days at Westminster were numbered and that with the new reign, new honours were to come to him, new spheres of influence and the loss maybe of peace of mind. Like the rest of England, he hoped for great things from the new sovereign, who was learned in theology and himself a scholar of no mean repute. The Queen was dead; long live the King.

III

THE AUTHORIZED VERSION
1604–1611

WHEN King James succeeded Elizabeth on the English throne, there seemed every reason to hope for many years of peace and prosperity. No longer need England fear invasion or rebellion or penury; her economic condition, her political stability alike gave cause for sober optimism. By 1603 the majority of Englishmen had accepted the Elizabethan Church, and were learning to love its liturgy, made familiar by regular and compulsory attendance at divine service. Discontent there was, and to spare, but it was hoped that King James would be able to pacify the critics and Francis Bacon, the greatest thinker of the age, had laid a paper before him indicating the wisest method of approach—a combination of order and clarity in essentials, with moderation and compromise in matters indifferent.

Yet despite these high hopes and good intentions in Church and State, within two brief years of James' accession, King and Parliament had drifted into complete disharmony. In the sphere of the Church, a number of zealous, God-fearing ministers had been silenced by an overbearing primate, while the Gunpowder Plot had shattered for centuries the hope of a closer understanding with Rome. No tranquil years awaited England in the immediate future. There was, however, after the stormy beginning, a hiatus of calm between the Gunpowder Treason and the death of Robert Cecil, Earl of Salisbury, who, as Secretary of State and Treasurer, maintained for a while the Tudor way of rule. In these quiet years there was a late flowering of the Elizabethan spirit, a triumphant *coda* to the symphony that had begun when the young Queen rode into London in 1558. In his preface to Andrewes' book of private prayers, Alexander Whyte, the Presbyterian divine, points out that the reign of James I, such a sorry business in so many ways, witnessed the production of three of the world's great masterpieces, Shakespeare's *King Lear*, Bacon's *Advancement of Learning*, and the Authorized Version of the Bible. With this latter, Lancelot Andrewes was immediately concerned and in these years he rose to a position of eminence at court.

As James and his Scottish train journeyed through England with spring blossoming on every hand to arrive at mid-summer at the gates of a London smitten with the Plague, petitioners of every kind assailed him. The group that interested him most were concerned with religious grievances; their petition bore a thousand names and they asked, among other things, that they might not be forced to wear the surplice and to use the cross in Baptism. The King assured them of his consideration and promised a conference on the disputed points. They might appear to be small points but they raised immediately the issue Elizabeth had tried to shelve; how far were questions of ceremonial and behaviour ' matters indifferent ' as Bacon urged; or how far were they the signs of a fundamental cleavage of opinion?

The latter was the point of view of Bancroft, Bishop of London, the chaplain and confidant of Archbishop Whitgift, who was prevented by increasing infirmity from taking any active share in the work of his office. Bancroft was a Lancashire man with a quick tongue and an equally quick brain, who could be gentle with his own clergy and dependants but who could never appreciate an opponent's point of view. He had a tidy mind and strong convictions and was anxious to reduce to some sort of order the conglomeration of undefined dogma and conflicting pronouncements which was the Elizabethan Church. But he failed to realize that it was this very

c

vagueness in non-essentials which made it possible for many
to conform who would be hard put to it if, in the interests of
consistency or principle, matters dubious were elucidated or
inconsistencies removed. Not that the faith of such men as
Bancroft and Andrewes was in any sense woolly or uncertain.
The *via media* was a path chosen deliberately as more likely
to lead to the truth than either extreme, a way of life, Catholic
in its respect for ancient custom, ordered worship and episcopal
rule, Protestant in its stress on the supremacy of the Scriptures,
interpreted according to the reasoned conclusion of the Church.
Andrewes was of more kindly temper than Bancroft, and
indeed, he had much in common with Bacon, whose lofty
wisdom was congenial to his own academic temper. In a sermon of a slightly later date he stressed the danger of too
arbitrary an approach. 'Those who have it all cut and dried,'
he asserted, 'sure must have been in God's cabinet above the
third Heaven where St. Paul never came.' But, as much as
Bancroft, he dreaded the growth of a host of varying opinions
and a steady progress in disorder. The desire for order and
discipline as a basic need of man and of society was one in
which Andrewes very fully shared. During that summer of
1603, preaching at Chiswick and watching with anxious eyes
the spread of the Plague in the city, he saw it as a punishment
for sin. 'By God's injunction we should all live,' he reminded
his fearful congregation, each looking askance at his neighbour
lest even in this river-side hamlet signs of the pestilence should
appear. 'And this injunction is,' he continued, 'you shall not
do every man what seems good in his own eyes (or finds out
in his own brains) but whatsoever I command you that only
shall you do. But we setting light by that charge of His, out
of the old disease of our father Adam, think it a goodly matter
to be witty, and to find out things ourselves, to make ourselves
to be authors and inventors of some what, that so we may
seem to be as wise as God, if not wiser, and to know what is
for our turns as well as He if not better.' This was the
temper which he thought responsible for innovations whether
in dress or in worship, linking together 'the new tricks,

opinions and fashions' of the dissentients of the Church with the 'new meats in diet and new fashions in apparel which men so dote on . . . as they care not what they spend on them'. Kindly as he was, it was not from Dean Andrewes that the Puritans could hope for comprehension.

Whether or not comprehension would grow out of further discussion was at best doubtful, but the King had great faith in his own powers of persuasion and the promised conference was summoned to meet at Hampton Court in the New Year of 1604. This elegant palace could challenge comparison with any of the royal houses that encircled London, not in size and grandeur but in the charm of its tangled chimneys, in the gardens, well planted with sweet-smelling herbs, and in the neighbouring Thames whose quiet waters, like the mercy of God, flowed steadily and strong to assuage the restlessness and ambition of men's hearts. Queen Anne, the new King's rather empty-headed Danish wife, had just spent her first English Christmas at Hampton Court, rediscovering her passion for amateur theatricals. Some of the precisians in the neighbouring borough of Kingston may have shaken their heads on hearing of the Queen's readiness to display her pink-and-white beauty in the less decorous parts of the Masque, but if so their equanimity was soon restored for, scarce were the Twelfth Night revels over, when there arrived at the Palace a most respectable company of learned divines and bustling bishops. Archbishop Whitgift could not come; he awaited daily a summons from a greater King than James. Bancroft was there and seven other bishops; there were eight deans, Andrewes among them, the King attended by his Privy Council, and four of the Puritan party. The King came to the conference with every intention of reaching an amicable agreement and in the preliminary discussion, at which the Puritans were not present, the tone of the meeting was conciliatory, and a compromise seemed possible on the lines suggested by Bacon. During the course of the second day's debate, the mood of the conference entirely changed. Of the four Puritans the learned Dr. Reynolds had been the obvious choice as spokesman, but it seemed to contemporaries that he did himself less than justice, while Ralph Knewstubs, his most vocal colleague, had no prudence to match his zeal. Three days sufficed to shatter every hope of harmony.

Reynolds began by pleading for the imposition of the Lambeth Articles which, at the very start, alienated the sympathy of men of Andrewes' way of thinking. Bancroft, who had few illusions as to the result of the conference, was in a state of perpetual irritation, and when Reynolds proceeded to criticize the confirmation service, he broke in with an angry interruption for which he was sternly reprimanded by the King. James himself was still hopeful and his optimism increased when the Puritans' next suggestion was a constructive one, a plea for a new translation of the Scriptures. Bancroft, however, was still critical. 'If every man's humour might be followed,' he muttered, 'there would be no end of translating.' He trembled for the result if the precisians started improving on the Bible. But James was enthusiastic. The translations should be 'done by the best learned in both universities, then reviewed by the Bishops, presented to the Privy Council, ratified by royal authority'. 'But it is fit that no marginal notes should be added thereunto,' Bancroft insisted, and James reassured him: 'That Caveat is well put in, for in the Geneva translation some notes are partial, untrue, seditious, and savouring of traitorous conceits. . . .' After a discussion on the danger of propaganda literature ('Popish and seditious pamphlets' hawked for sale in Paul's Churchyard), the fatigued participants came out into the dusk of the January afternoon, with something accomplished but no growing sense of fellowship to protect them when they plunged next day into controversial matter.

In the morning Reynolds began with an earnest plea for learned ministers in every parish, touching Bancroft on the raw, for no one was more conscious than he of the deficiency of the Church in this respect. The King reminded Reynolds that Jerusalem could not be built in a day, and that not only was there a lack of suitable ordinands but that there was not sufficient money to maintain them. Bancroft, kneeling before the King, perhaps as a sign of the renewed humility of spirit in which he had begun the fresh day, interposed with a suggestion showing the different orientation of the two parties. He pleaded: 'That there may be amongst us a praying ministry, it being now come to pass that men think it is the only duty of ministers to spend their time in the pulpit.' 'Good homilies' were, however, suggested as a temporary expedient till sufficient learned men were forthcoming who were able to preach.

This type of criticism was constructive and helpful. Up to this point the conference might be said to have been successful. But the protagonists had only been skirting round the real points at issue and now Reynolds proceeded to the vexed subject of the use of the cross in the baptismal service. The Puritans objected strongly to this as a 'popish custom'; Bancroft's argument was that its ancient usage went back to the early Church and was a part of the Catholic tradition in which they all shared. How long had it been used, asked Reynolds, and it was Andrewes who was able to give the answer—'it appears out of Tertullian, Cyprian and Origen that it was used *in immortali lavacro*'. 'In Constantine's time,' added one of the bishops, more succinctly. That being so, said the King, there was no reason why the Church should not continue the custom. But Dr. Reynolds began to talk about papal abuses, murmuring something about the brazen serpent. The King interrupted him. 'Inasmuch as the cross was abused to superstition in time of popery,' he argued, 'it doth plainly imply that it was well used before', and in a burst of temper that should have warned the petitioners to be careful he added: 'I detest their courses who peremptorily disallow of all things which have been abused in popery.'

Here was the crux of the whole matter; the determination of those in authority to go behind papal abuses to the ancient custom of the Church, to remain at all costs Catholic and Reformed; the Puritans' desire for a complete break with all they equated with Popery and their fear that severity would

lead to secession. Knewstubs spoke finely of Christian liberty
in the impassioned speech in which he now pleaded against
the imposition of a uniform ceremonial. But James had
heard a similar argument at the last conference on religion he
had attended in Scotland, when a young clergyman, 'a beard-
less boy', had expressed himself ready to conform in doctrine
but had demanded freedom in matters of ceremony. 'But I
will have none of that,' cried James. 'I will have one doctrine,
one discipline, one religion in substance and in ceremony.
Never speak more to that point, how far you are bound to
obey.'

Just when the King was reflecting sourly that there was little
to choose between these English Puritans and the mentors of
his youth, someone rashly mentioned Presbyterianism. James
broke out into an angry torrent of words which not only
ruined all hope of success at Hampton Court, but boded ill
for the future of himself and England. A presbytery, he
asserted, would agree as well with monarchy as God and the
devil. 'Then Jack and Tom and Will and Dick shall meet
and at their pleasure censure me and my Council and all our
proceedings. . . .' What he said was true. There was no
hope of compromise between his theory of sovereignty and
the new political ideas that were developing out of Calvinist
theology, but the conference was ruined by the sudden trans-
formation of the impartial chairman he had originally set out
to be into a heated and indignant protagonist threatening, if
the dissidents did not agree, to harry them out of the land.
The delegates met next day with a realization of the all but
unbearable truth that unity of Christian faith and worship
had been shattered by the Reformation and the fifty years
that followed, in a way that could not be plastered up by any
three-day conference.

The Puritans had still a little fight left in them. Turning
from the general to the particular, Mr. Chaderton put in a
special plea for the Vicar of Rochdale, whose conscience was
tender on the points under debate, but whose piety and able
preaching had alone prevented that part of Lancashire from

reverting entirely to Popery. Someone pointed out that others had been offended by the vicar's casual way of handing round the bread in an open basket when he administered communion. James, however, was in better humour this morning and he promised that the vicar's idiosyncrasies should be treated gently, whereupon Knewstubs raised the question of some honest ministers in Suffolk who disliked the surplice, and James' impatience began to return; were there always to be exceptions and never unwavering obedience? He dismissed the conference which ended with nothing to its credit save the proposed translation, and with a knowledge of the cleavage between the parties which the King had brought home to all concerned in the most infelicitous and unconciliatory way. Dean Andrewes had not opened his mouth except on the one occasion, but it is only fair to add that he found himself in entire agreement with the King's main decisions, his refusal to impose the Articles, his insistence on ordered worship and his intention to maintain in that worship as many as possible of the ancient rites of the early Church. With regard to the translation, he was the natural chairman of a group engaged in the project who were to meet at Westminster, and as early as November 1604, he excused himself from a meeting of the Society of Antiquaries in the words, ' But that this afternoon is our translation time and most of our company are negligent I would have seen you '.

The King had issued clear instructions as to how he wished the work to be done and Andrewes' good opinion of his scholarship and piety grew as he had further proof of the royal insistence on accuracy and respect for Holy Writ. Bancroft's dislike of marginal notes was repeated and stressed by the King in his instructions to the translators. As far as possible existent translations were to be used; the Bishops' Bible, dating from 1568, was to be given priority, with reference to Tyndale's and Coverdale's earlier versions when necessary. The original Greek and Hebrew were to be consulted and to secure this forty-seven of the leading scholars of the country were empanelled. They were to form themselves into six groups, meeting at Westminster, Oxford and Cambridge, and each group was to deal with a certain section of the Scriptures. The proceedings were to be as follows: 'every particular man of each company to take the same chapter or chapters, and having translated or amended them severally by himself where he thinks good, all to meet together, confer what they have done and agree for their part what shall stand.' The agreed version was then sent round the other five groups for their approval and any criticisms or emendations then suggested were to be considered at a final meeting of the chairmen of all six groups.

Lancelot Andrewes, whose eminence as a scholar of Hebrew made him an obvious choice, was chairman of one of the Westminster groups, to which was allotted the books of the Old Testament, from the beginning of Genesis to the end of the second book of Kings. Another member of this group was Dr. Laifield, the Parson of St. Clement Danes, who was specially included because 'being skilled in architecture his judgment was much relied on for the fabric of the tabernacle and temple'. There were a good many preliminaries to be settled and it was some little while before the work really got started. There was a fresh delay when Mr. Lively of Cambridge died suddenly, for he was a specialist in Oriental tongues whose expert knowledge could not easily be replaced. Indeed the progress, as always, was slower than was expected and there was no shortage of captious critics able to detect some ulterior motive in the delay. 'However the rest vigorously and slowly proceeded in this hard, heavy and holy task, nothing offended with the censures of impatient people, condemning their delays (though indeed but due deliberation) for laziness.' Thus Fuller records in his Church History.

At long last, in 1611, the agreed version was ready to be presented to the King, with a rather fulsome dedication, drawn up by the Cambridge scholar, Dr. Smith, which makes one thankful that the text itself is free of glosses and that no contemporary political theory or ecclesiastical divergence has been allowed to mar its beauty. For miraculously this small company of dedicated men had produced a masterpiece, and it was the very subjugation of individuality upon which Bancroft had insisted from the start, which gave the translation its abiding value. Each person in the team had given fully and freely of his scholarship and piety but no self assertion, no striving after originality, intruded itself to lessen for posterity the potency and relevance of this authorized version of the Scriptures. For his share in this achievement, much can be forgiven to King James. One cannot be sufficiently thankful that just at the time when the English language was at its finest and most expressive and when the spiritual faculties of its most learned practitioners were exceptionally acute, a King should ordain and see accomplished this mighty undertaking. The work was carried out by men immersed at other hours in multifarious duties in Church and State; it must have used up over a space of years their energy and leisure and time that they might have spent on their own literary compositions; they derived from it neither fame nor fortune; and it does indeed seem that the Holy Spirit of God accepted their sacrifice and worked through them to give to all who speak the English tongue a possession of lasting and imperishable worth.

Thus at Westminster, in the ancient Jerusalem chamber, Lancelot Andrewes and his colleagues drenched themselves anew in the pages of the Old Testament, and told again the great story of the Creation which never ceased to be for him a special source of wonder and worship. The figures of the Patriarchs, the journey through the wilderness, Israel's anointed Kings, seemed at times more real than the life which went on beyond the Abbey precincts. But in that world without, Andrewes himself had an ever-increasing part to play. Once again he had been offered a bishopric, and there were no degrading financial conditions to justify refusal. King James was sound on the question of lay impropriations, even though his shortage of funds prevented him effectively from putting matters right.

Andrewes knew that promotion would mean a further immersion in public affairs, though he did not realize that he would be plunged in the controversies not only of England but of Europe. He was, however, less conscious than most men of the tension between the things of the spirit and practical life. His life was passed *sub specie aeternitatis* and every action was done to the glory of God. It was with his usual cheerful serenity that he accepted the see of Chichester, and was consecrated in the autumn of 1605, saying farewell with regret to Westminster and cutting the ties which had bound him for so many years to Cambridge and the city of London, when he resigned the cure of St. Giles and the Mastership of Pembroke. About the same time the King made him the Royal Almoner, a post for which his shrewdness and sympathy, his common sense and deep compassion, particularly fitted him. For the next twenty years he was well known and well loved at Whitehall, a familiar figure on all State occasions, yet never quite belonging to his surroundings. For the hours of prayer with which he began his day seemed to clothe him in a garment of sanctity and amid so much that was hollow and petty and vicious, his charity and kindliness in human relationships made men at once ashamed and thankful. And always through the discordant noises of the court and the sweet harmony of his own spiritual life, there sounded the ground bass of the Old Testament Scriptures, conditioning alike his worship and his thought. An unwavering faith in a righteous God, and a sad tendency to equate King James with the Kings of Israel who had served that righteous God, made him at once sublime in his spiritual strength and strangely remiss in his political acumen. Happily for us the politics are a thing of the past, while the prayers that were alike the fruits and the sustenance of that saintly pilgrimage remain as signposts still for the pilgrims of to-day.

IV

CONSPIRACY AND CONTROVERSY
1605–10

LANCELOT ANDREWES was consecrated Bishop of Chichester on Sunday, November 3rd, 1605. The new session of Parliament was due to meet after various postponements on November 5th. On that day he would be qualified to take his place among the peers of the realm of England; and it must have been with a consciousness of new responsibilities and great opportunities that he retired to rest on the previous night. But before it was light an incredible tale had got abroad; a dastardly conspiracy had been discovered, kegs of gunpowder beneath the House of Lords, which, but for God's providence, would that very day have been blown sky high with the King and the Prince, the Parliament assembled and even the ladies watching the opening ceremony. Andrewes was horrified, sickened by the very thought of what had been intended. It made upon him, as upon all his contemporaries, an indelible impression, and in his case duty as well as emotion directed his thoughts towards it for many years to come, alike in his capacity as preacher of commemoration sermons and as the protagonist of the Church of England in the paper warfare with Rome which it engendered.

The story of the plot is one of heroism twisted awry, religion transformed into ruthless fanaticism, self-devotion which did not stop at murder. It germinated in the restlessness of Robert Catesby, a Roman Catholic of good estate and reputation, who would have welcomed an invasion from Spain in 1603 and who

43

now, disappointed in his hopes of leniency from James,
planned to seize the government by force, following up the
explosion at Westminster by armed revolt in Warwickshire.
The men he gathered round him, his cousin Thomas Winter,
John Wright his friend and Thomas Percy, the Earl of Northumberland's kinsman, regarded themselves as dedicated men.
For eighteen months they kept the secret of the plot, living
their normal lives in public, while they hired cellars in Westminster, dug tunnels and stored gunpowder, their numbers
increasing dangerously as the need for money and for men
who could dig necessitated more accomplices. But for the
repeated adjournments of Parliament they might well have
succeeded. As it was, at the eleventh hour, a conspirator sent
to a friend a warning letter which fell into Cecil's hands. The
cellars were searched and the soldier Guy Fawkes, who gave
his name as Johnson, was discovered mounting guard over the
gunpowder. The other conspirators fled to Warwickshire,
taking refuge at last in a country house at Holbeche where
many were shot down. The rest, less fortunate, were brought
to London for a speedy trial and execution.

Upon its first discovery, the horror of the plot struck home
to every heart. This was worse than the fires of Smithfield;
here was Bartholomew's massacre, repeated and enhanced;
this devilry spared not the King himself nor the most innocent
witness of the scene. It was the suddenness of the intended
destruction which appalled men; for even the veriest criminal
on the scaffold, the wretch dying in the gutter of the Plague,
had the chance to repent, to cry upon God with his dying
breath, to plead the wounds of Christ. But here, as Andrewes
put it in one of his sermons, there was to be no brand plucked
from the burning, no pulling out of the fire, no saving any,
and to him with his acute sense of God's judgment and of
the sinfulness of the best of men this was indeed terrible.

He heard of his own narrow escape in the early hours of
November 5th when, in his own words, 'a great part of us
were not out of our beds and scarce well awake'. The news
spread through the city and there ensued such a pealing of

bells as had not been heard within the memory of man; the streets blazed with bonfires, and men recalled that now for the second time the King had escaped a direct attack upon his sacred person. Five years before, on another Tuesday, again on the 5th of the month (though in August not November) at a place called Johnstown (and Guy Fawkes had called himself Johnson) the two sons of the Earl of Gowrie, who had been executed during the King's minority, had attempted to avenge their father by killing James. Only the momentary hesitation of one of them had enabled the King to escape. So close had he been, twice, to death.

Up and down the streets of London excited tongues buzzed, and even the elderly and respectable news-writer, John Chamberlain (a university friend of Bishop Andrewes), reported the coincidence to his correspondent, Sir Dudley Carleton, the Ambassador at the Hague. Two days later when Parliament met, it was ordained that there should be special sermons each year to commemorate the royal escapes, on August 5th, the anniversary of the Gowrie conspiracy, and on November 5th, that 'Gunpowder Treason should never be forgot'. During the years that followed it was Lancelot Andrewes who preached the greater number of these sermons, at Whitehall in November, but in August at one or other of the places where the King stayed on his summer progress, at Burghley, at Okham, at Holdenby, where in 1610 Knollys reported that the fifth of August had passed with mirth and an excellent sermon from the Bishop.

Andrewes' detestation of the plot went deeper than a mere horror of physical violence. Some months after the first executions, Garnet, the Superior of the Jesuits in England, was brought to trial. How much he knew of the plot, before its outlines were revealed to him under the seal of confession, remains one of the enigmas of history; his condemnation was a foregone conclusion in spite of his able defence and he did his cause little good by a paper, in which under certain circumstances he had justified equivocation, a detail which gave Shakespeare a good line in his new tragedy of *Macbeth*.

Andrewes was deeply impressed by Garnet's trial, and the thing which sickened him most was the manner in which a cloak of religion had been drawn over the whole diabolical scheme. The first joint action of the conspirators had been to receive the sacrament. At the end Catesby had died kissing the feet of the Virgin; young Rokewood, drawn on his hurdle down the Strand, had called bravely to his wife to pray for his soul. 'Undertaken with a holy oath, bound with the holy sacrament'; Andrewes was horror stricken. 'This shrining it, such an abomination, setting it in the holy place, so ugly and odious, making such a treason as this, a religious missal, sacramental treason, hallowing it with orison, oath and eucharist; this passeth all the rest.' This was sacrilege, and sacrilege was a sin from which Andrewes, with his vigorous sense of God's sovereignty, shrank with particular abhorrence. There is no sign of the tenderness for which he was famed in those parts of his sermons which deal with the conspirators.

There was another aspect of the two conspiracies which raised a problem that became with every year more pressing and more controversial. The Plots had involved an attack on the King's person, upon the Lord's anointed! Could any circumstance justify any such rebellion; was not the sovereign by virtue of his office possessed of a *jus divinum*, which set him above the laws, which made obedience not merely a civil duty but a religious obligation? The whole vexed question of authority was raised by this enquiry, and it was this that Andrewes endeavoured to answer in his commemoration sermons. He himself had no doubts on the matter and those who listened to him listened with approval. Monarchical power was a thing from God: not yet had Thomas Hobbes, Bacon's eccentric secretary, enunciated his disturbing theory that the power of the ruler was based on a contract between himself and the ruled. Andrewes shared with Hooker and Bancroft a high conception of kingship analogous to that of the Lord's anointed in Old Testament history. 'If, with approbation from Heaven,' Hooker had asked, 'the Kings of God's chosen people had in the affairs of Jewish religion supreme power, why not Christian Kings the like power in Christian countries?' Andrewes embellished the theme in his denunciations of rebellion. 'But they that rise against the King are God's enemies for God and the King are so in a league, such a knot, so straight between them as one cannot be the enemy to the one but he must be to the other. . . . Moses' rod, God's; Gideon's sword, God's; David's throne, God's. In His place they sit, His Person they represent, they are taken into the fellowship of the same name.'

Here was hard doctrine indeed, especially when in place of David there was James Stuart. But Andrewes argued (in that very sermon of 1610 which Knollys commended) that obedience was due not to the person but to the office of king; not because 'he is virtuous, religious or wise but because he is "Christus Domini". . . God saith not "Touch him not, he is a good Catholic, or endued with this virtue or that. Touch him not; he deserveth well, or at least doth no harm." No, these would fail He saw or be said to fail though they failed not. We should never then have done, never have been quiet. . . .' In that last sentence lay the root of the matter. Logically and intellectually, the theory of the King's divine right appealed to Andrewes, in part because of the Old Testament parallel, in part because of his conviction that there must be in ecclesiastical as in secular matters an effective central authority, which would fulfil the functions previously exercised by the Pope. But his whole-hearted acceptance of the principle was largely an emotional matter. He disliked intensely the 'new parity and confusion of the Anabaptists'. 'We should never then have done, never have been quiet.' And order and tranquillity were to him the essentials of well-being, whether in the furnishing of his chapel or the conduct of the realm. Living daily a life of Christian discipline, he believed that the duty to obey was of God, and his conception of the universe was of an ordered hierarchy in which each man rested content in that state of life to which it should please God to call him. Only of recent years had England established the supremacy of law; in Scotland, as James could witness, ordered living was yet far to seek. The provision of security was the first requisite in an age which had witnessed once again in the Gunpowder treason the irruption of force through the thin veneer of civilization. It seemed to many good Christians of that generation that the duty of obedience, the virtues of law and order, were not only more immediately relevant than the cultivation of freedom, but were indeed the essential framework without which there could be no freedom. Andrewes' adoption of this unhappy theory of the divine right of kings, which was destined to bring war upon England and James' successor to the scaffold, was thus rather a matter of religion than political theory. It was part and parcel of the man, however out of sympathy we may be with it to-day, and explains in large measure his compliance with the King's wishes throughout his twenty years at court, a compliance that came the more readily because of his personal regard for James, for whom he continued to have a genuine admiration and affection.

The tie that bound the Bishop and the King was that of scholarship, for Andrewes was a learned man and a theologian, and James loved learning and regarded theology not only as the queen of sciences but as one in which he himself did not lack proficiency. In knowledge, as in so much else, the age was one of transition. There were men of genius, like Francis Bacon and the robust and genial Dr. Harvey, who were experimenting with new scientific methods and were impatient of the lawyers' preoccupation with precedents and the theologians' Thomist philosophy. On the Continent, Galileo was following truth courageously down strange paths, and the day was not far distant when the Church would give him solemn warning that the conclusions he reached were contrary to Holy Writ and 'manifestly absurd'. But in England the King's own predilections and the earnest desire of the bishops to give the ecclesiastical settlement those roots in the past, without which in conservative England it could not hope to survive, kept many of the best brains in the country (to Bacon's disgust) intent on the work of combating the Counter-Reformation and evolving a theology that would fit a Church,

Catholic but Reformed. As usual in England, the first approach to the problem had been pragmatical. The Gunpowder Plot had once more drawn attention to the vexed question of the political loyalty of the Papists, and in an attempt to distinguish between those Catholics who wished to live 'in civil obedience' and those who were potential rebels, an oath of allegiance had been introduced to be tendered as required. For all his cleverness, James never learnt to be wise. The oath forced an issue that had been better left unspecified and Catholics compelled to choose between disloyalty to their King and the denial of an accepted tenet of their Church, the Papacy's right of deposition, found themselves in an impossible position.

George Blackwell, the doyen of the English priests, at first professed himself ready to take the oath and ignored a *breve* issued from Rome which forbade subscription. He longed only for tranquillity. So did hundreds of loyal Catholics, the Blundells in Lancashire, the Staffordshire Gerrards, the tenants of the Howards in Sussex and elsewhere. Often they were left in passable quiet for long periods at a time, but it was never security; some twist in foreign affairs, some rumour of conspiracy, some change in the delicate balance of court favour and the recusancy laws would again be put into execution. This was what happened after the discovery of the Gunpowder Plot and it was the context of the oath of allegiance in a mass of legislation so clearly intended to 'rid the Kingdom of these pestiferous adversaries', to use Bancroft's own unguarded words, that made Rome adamant, though the English Catholics, if left to themselves, might by some sort of compromise have achieved a measure of stability.

A second *breve* from the Vatican shattered any such hope. At the same time, Cardinal Bellarmine, the great controversialist now resident in Rome, wrote categorically to Blackwell under the Pope's direction censuring his attitude and condemning the oath, because 'it tends to this end that the authority of the head of the Church in England may be transferred from the succession of St. Peter to the succession of

King Henry the 8th '. Thereupon, King James, under a thin veil of anonymity, published an *Apology for the Oath*, by no means devoid of learning and acumen, in which he distinguished between the oath of supremacy which dealt with the King's powers in ecclesiastical matters and the oath of allegiance which was an emergency matter intended only to test his subjects' loyalty.

And now the flood-gates of controversy opened. In September 1608, a reply to the *Apology* bore the name *Responsio Matthaei Torti*, and since Matthew Tortus was the name of one of Bellarmine's household servants, one had not far to seek for the true author. It was a shock for James, for good amateur theologian though he was, he stood little chance against the Jesuit, Bellarmine, who for many years had held the chair of controversial theology in Rome. James set about feverishly revising his *Apology* and Bishop Andrewes was called in to assist him.

That was an uncomfortable autumn for all concerned. The court could not leave Whitehall till the job was done, and Andrewes compared the work of revision to Penelope's web ' for what he had finished at night His Majesty undid it in the morning '. The King's temper was frayed and Matthew Tortus' *Responsio* was solemnly burnt at Paul's Cross while, in addition to revising the *Apology*, James instructed Andrewes to write under his own name a complete confutation of Bellarmine's work.

The newswriter Chamberlain commented to Dudley Carleton that he was doubtful how Andrewes would undertake and perform the task, it ' being so contrary to his disposition and course to meddle with controversie '. On November 11th in a further letter Chamberlain again referred to the preoccupation of ' the good Bishop of Chichester '; ' the King doth so hasten and spur him on in this business of Bellarmine's which he were likely to perform very well (as I hear by them that can judge) if he might take his own time and not be entangled with arguments obtruded to him continually by the King '. Even so, the finished work was regarded by Carleton as ' worthy ' though, he added, 'the brevity breeds obscurity and puts the reader to some of the pains which were taken by the writer '.

The King's *Apology* was re-issued in May 1609 and Andrewes' *Tortura Torti* appeared in June. All through the summer of 1609 Bellarmine sweated in a hot room in the Vatican, composing his reply, just as Andrewes had shivered in London during the preceding winter. The Cardinal's *Apology for the Responsio* was issued under his own name and, in its turn, evoked in 1610 a further reply or *Responsio* from Andrewes, 'five hundred crochety pages ', as they appear to Bellarmine's modern biographer,[1] yet approved among others by Isaac Casaubon, the great Swiss scholar who came that year to England and saw in them an exposition of the Church he desired, midway between Rome and Luther, with firm historical foundations, a sacramental framework, and room for independence of thought.

The controversy was of its time, marred by personal invective which comes unhappily from the pens of two gentle and kindly scholars who, had they met, would have found they had much in common. They were of the same age and both of comparatively humble origin. Bellarmine had been born in the little hill town of Montepulciano whence he had ridden to Rome as a youth of eighteen to join the Jesuit order, and from that time on had been a man under discipline. He passed seven years in Belgium, and from 1576-88 achieved such fame as the spokesman of the Counter-Reformation that his name became a by-word throughout the length and breadth of Europe. He had even given his name to a special sort of full-bellied jug which the designer claimed to resemble him; though in England they said it had gained that name because an undergraduate, hiding a jug of beer beneath his gown, when challenged by his tutor as to what he concealed promptly answered 'Bellarmine' whose *Controversies* were among the reading matter of every conscientious student.

From Belgium and France Bellarmine was called back to

---

[1] See Jas. Brodrick, S.J., *Life and Works of Cardinal Bellarmine*, II, p. 226 *et alia*.

Rome where at the English college he had taught the young men, who came over under Campion's leadership to win back England to the old allegiance. Yet this Lion of the Church was a man of intense humility. A visitor to Rome in 1580 wrote: 'When I was engaged with him in the service of the kitchen and in washing and drying dishes, he did all this lowly work as energetically, carefully and exactly as if it were the big business of theology that occupied him and never a word did he speak or once look round.' When some years later the deserved and expected honour of a Cardinal's hat was offered to Bellarmine, he accepted with tears and only after a stern reminder of his duty of obedience. To a friend who congratulated him he wrote: 'I thank you very heartily for your kindness and I excuse your mistake. Believe me, the only feeling I have about my elevation is one of anxiety and fright at the extreme danger in which it has placed me.' It was in that same spirit that Andrewes accepted his first bishopric. Alas, that within a few years the Bishop and the Cardinal were attacking each other with the darts of their irony and the heavy artillery of invective.

In so far as the immediate subject of debate was the oath of allegiance, the controversy raised again the vexed question of sovereign power, a matter on which Bellarmine's views were notoriously heterodox. For he based the right of the temporal ruler upon 'the taut or express command of the ruled', a foreshadowing of the idea of contract, for which Andrewes had only a scathing reply. The latter, however, proceeded to examine the extent and nature of the royal supremacy in a manner which lifted the *Tortura* above the level of ephemeral dispute. The influence of the philosophical thought of the day is seen in his appeal to the law of nature. 'This is a theological certainty and agreed upon by all that Christ did not come to invert or displace the order either of nature or of society.' The claim of kings to allegiance is in fact like the parental right, an element in the natural order of the world.[1] How

---

[1] Ottley, *Lancelot Andrewes*, p. 63, and cf. pp. 150-76, for an excellent summary of Andrewes' theological position.

characteristic of Andrewes is this stress on order, on the idea of fulfilment rather than of revolution!

Andrewes, according to Chamberlain, considered Bellarmine's second tract, *The Apology*, to be a work of no great account. Either the Cardinal was 'crazed' [sick] or treated his subject with 'contemptuous negligence'. He had changed his line of attack and now concentrated on the question of whether any man could call himself a Catholic who did not believe in transubstantiation and other specific dogmas. This gave Andrewes a chance in his *Responsio* to voice the conviction very dear to his heart, that the accepted doctrine of the Christian Church of primitive times, the fundamentals embodied in the historic Creeds, alone composed the *Fide Catholica*, to which during the Middle Ages numerous accretions had been added of varying worth and beauty, but none 'necessary to Salvation'. 'Our religion,' he wrote, 'you miscall modern sectarian opinions. I tell you if they are modern, they are not ours; our appeal is to antiquity.' Some years later he enlarged upon this theme in some letters to the French Cardinal Perron, who had taken up the cudgels on Bellarmine's behalf in correspondence with Casaubon, and it is from these writings that Andrewes' conception of the Holy Catholic Church becomes evident. Once in a sermon he stressed again in characteristic phrase this dependence of the English Church upon primitive Christianity. The boundary of our Faith was to be found, he said, in 'one Canon reduced to writing by God himself, two testaments, three creeds, four general councils, five centuries, and the series of Fathers in that period'. In this heritage eastern and western Churches shared alike, and when the mists of controversy had cleared away, Andrewes' prayers remained prayers for the Church Universal, for a healing of schism throughout the world and for his own British Church, 'that what was lacking might be provided'.

V

SCHISM AND HERESY
1605-11

IT IS ALWAYS a Cathedral town, wrote F. V. Lucas of
Chichester. 'Whatever noise may be in the air you know in
your heart that quietude is its true characteristic. One might
say that above the loudest street cries you are continually
conscious of the silence of the close.' So it is to-day; so it must
have been when Lancelot Andrewes was Bishop of the diocese
that stretched from the Channel to the flat country beyond
the Downs. Chichester still retains within its ancient walls a
measure of its former shape and nature, its four roads meeting
at the market cross, with the fair proportions of the Cathedral
gracing the south-west corner of the town. In this enclave,
which during Andrewes' tenure of the see came directly under
the Bishop's jurisdiction, episcopal palace, Dean's house and
ecclesiastical residences of varying shapes and sizes still stand
in an area of serene loveliness, of green lawns and flowering
trees and a tangle of red roofs. Here Andrewes came at inter-
vals during the four years of his episcopacy and he must have
rejoiced in the beauty of worship to be found in a Cathedral
whose organist in 1608 was Thomas Weelkes, the writer of
madrigals. How often he visited Chichester it is not easy to
compute. The greater part of his time must have been spent
at his town house in the parish of St. Martins within Ludgate,
for both the controversial writings and his duties as King's
Almoner kept him much at court. He probably spent the
summer months, when James was on progress, in visiting his

54

diocese where, in addition to the visitation of the parishes, the confirmation of children and the dedication of churches, he must have given some time and attention to the administration of the episcopal enclave, with the many matters such as the repair of the city wall over which there was apt to be friction. He already knew Lord Lumley, the chief landowner in the neighbourhood, as a fellow-member of the Society of Antiquaries. Perhaps he went occasionally to Arundel where the castle of the Howards stood above the gap, though the fierce Catholicism of the old Countess of Arundel precludes the likelihood of many friendly visits. The young Earl, however, who was Lumley's brother-in-law, had inherited his father's interest in matters intellectual and in many ways the tone of the great house would be congenial to Andrewes.

In 1609 as a reward for his labours on the *Tortura* he was translated to the bishopric of Ely, a wealthy and important diocese in a part of England he had known and loved in his Cambridge days. His sermon at Whitehall that Christmas was on the theme of fulness, and truly at this time life was full for Bishop Andrewes. He was at the height of his powers, on easy terms with old friends and new, in a court that had not yet entirely lost the spaciousness of Elizabethan days. He was fond of his new diocese, which brought him once again in close touch with the university, and indeed he had only one regret, that he found the climate of the fen country did not suit him in the winter months and he could spend less time there than he would have wished. He was accustomed, however, to pass the summer at Downham, his country residence, while for the greater part of the rest of the year he lived in London as before, at the Bishop's town house in Holborn.

Ely Place was one of the grandest and most famous of the great episcopal palaces that had once been so numerous in the city. Its garden was a source of pride to every Londoner who loved beauty and Shakespeare was sure of a response from the groundlings when, in his *Richard III*, he made Gloucester address the Bishop of Ely:

'When I was last in Holborn
I saw good strawberries in your garden there
I do beseech you send for some of them.'

In 1576 Christopher Hatton had cast greedy eyes on Ely
Place, and the then Bishop Cox had been forced to lease to
Hatton a large part of his estate, including the garden and
the gatehouse, for the annual rent of a rose, a cartload of hay
and the sum of £10. The only grace the Bishop could obtain
was permission to gather every summer a bushel of the roses.
After Hatton's death the land remained in the possession of
his widow, a quarrelsome lady who met her match in her
second husband, Sir Edward Coke, and who was still alive
during Andrewes' tenure of the see. The boundary between
her portion of Ely Place and the part which still belonged to
the Bishop was marked by a cherry tree in the garden of the
Mitre Tavern which still stands to-day.

Andrewes had what mattered most to him in the chapel, and
he set about making it what he thought a chapel should be, en-
riching its ceremonial out of his knowledge of ancient custom
and the ritual of the eastern Church, and maintaining standards
of reverence and dignity, in the conviction that the respect
shown to a King in his court should at least be equalled in
the worship of God in His Church. Years later, the uncom-
promising Prynne gave a description of Bishop Andrewes'
private chapel, retailing in scorn the candlesticks upon the
altar, the canister for wafers, the basin and ewer towel, the
censer and the copes, and the 'Romish furniture' of chancel
and side-chapel. But Andrewes' loyal secretary, Isaacson,
came nearer to the spirit of the place when he commented,
'Yea some that had been there were so taken with it that they
desired to end their days in the Bishop of Ely's chapel'.

The lovely Gothic building still stands, for happily it has
survived alike the ravages of progress and of war. There have
been many vicissitudes since Andrewes practised there the
beauty of holiness. After his translation to Winchester, Ely
Place was for four years the private chapel of Count Gondo-

mar, the Spanish Ambassador. After his departure the chapel reverted to the Bishops of Ely till the latter moved to a new home in Piccadilly in 1772, and later it was used in turn by the National Society for preaching the Gospel to the Poor and by a body of Welsh Episcopalians, until in 1874 it was sold by public auction to a Roman Catholic Society, the Fathers of Charity. Now in its retired corner of the city, battered but not destroyed by bombing, it stands as a witness to continuing Christian faith, and one would like to think that in the quiet fields of Paradise, all arguments stilled before the one abiding fact of Christ's atoning love, Lancelot Andrewes and Robert Bellarmine look down together on those who are restoring 'the Bishop of Ely's' chapel to a dignity and beauty worthy of the worship of God.

Andrewes remained Bishop of Ely for eight years during which time he was seldom absent from any occasion of importance at Whitehall, where the bishops under the leadership of Bancroft, who had succeeded Whitgift in the Primacy, still retained something of their medieval character as political magnates. But Andrewes went without any consciousness of abrupt transition from an audience with the King to wash the feet of poor men at Ely Place on Maundy Thursday, or used his money as readily to contribute generously to a free gift of the clergy to the Crown, or to further anonymously the welfare of a poor scholar. He preached incessantly, maintained a steady output of theological writing, filled his days to the full with public and private business, and whatever his occupations, never failed to pray. Amid the various changes and factions of court life, he had only one rule, to bear witness to the need for unity and accord, declaring that the Holy Spirit could only enter into the life of the individual or the community if there were harmony to be found. 'There is not a greater bar, a more fatal or forcible opposition to His entry than discord or disunited minds.' He spoke this in a sermon of 1606 and it was the keynote of his life. The men at James' court listened and revered him, and then all too often went their discordant way.

When Archbishop Bancroft died in the late autumn of 1610, the Bishop of Ely was confidently named as his successor, as the natural heir to the tradition to which Matthew Parker, Whitgift and Bancroft had each in their way contributed. Indeed, Andrewes himself seemed the only person not non-plussed when his claims were overlooked, and in February 1611 the King's choice fell on George Abbot, who barely a year before had become Bishop of London, and who had been the chaplain of James' Scottish favourite, Lord Dunbar.

Abbot was a few years younger than Andrewes, the son of a Guildford cloth-worker and one of a sturdy independent brood who were educated at the local grammar school, whence at the age of sixteen, he went up to Balliol, taking with him a love of his home town that he never lost, the highest standards of rectitude, and a somewhat forbidding manner in the presence of persons or things with which he did not agree. Abbot remained at Oxford for many years, entering holy orders in 1585, and becoming Master of University College and three times Vice-Chancellor. But, like Andrewes, he was not destined to an academic career, and after James' accession, as chaplain first to the Earl of Dorset and then to Dunbar, he became well known at Whitehall and was consecrated Bishop of London about the same time that Andrewes was translated to Ely.

At Oxford, Abbot's sturdy Protestantism agreed well with the Calvinism dominant in the university before Laud began to trouble the waters. It also recommended him to the Scots when he went north with Dunbar in 1608. James, disappointed in his hopes of a political union between Scotland and England, hoped to establish an effective episcopacy north of the Tweed which might mark the beginning of real spiritual unity. Abbot contributed not a little to reconciling the General Assembly to the royal policy. There was a rigidity alike about his theology and his morals which appealed to the Scottish clergy and made them less mistrustful of their English brethren. Three of them even agreed to come to London and to be consecrated by three English bishops, of whom Andrewes was one. But the latter was uneasy, for he was doubtful whether the Scots should not first have been ordained according to Anglican rites. Obviously Abbot was a man more fitted to the King's purpose at this crucial moment. When Bancroft died in the autumn of 1610 Dunbar urged James to appoint Abbot as his successor, but before a decision was made Dunbar also died. Those who thought that this spoilt Abbot's chances forgot the tenacity of the King's affections. The appointment had become not merely a matter of expediency for the furtherance of the Scottish scheme, but also an obligation to be honoured and a gesture to the memory of a dead friend.

In February Abbot became Archbishop, and set about to pursue honestly and vigorously his rather lonely way through the labyrinths of the court. He was a man of sterner mould than Andrewes, and James may well have regarded the latter as too yielding in temper for the stormy office of Primate. But his decision did not prove to be a happy one, for Abbot, who had never had any pastoral experience, failed to win the love and allegiance of his clergy, and he stood apart from that rich flowering of Anglican faith and worship, to which Donne and George Herbert, Nicholas Ferrar and Andrewes himself all in their different ways contributed.

Andrewes bore no ill-will to the new Archbishop and was well content as he was. After 1611, the main body of his controversial work and his labours on the translation were completed. King James had now another matter in hand, though not one destined to the same success. He wished to found a college of divines, which should carry on the work which Andrewes had begun in the *Tortura* and would serve as a 'spiritual garrison' permanently engaged in theological study and debate. In May 1610 he obtained from the Earl of Nottingham a stretch of land in Chelsea by the side of the river Thames. But the expenses of building proved prodigious, the Dean of Exeter, whom James appointed Provost, was morose and unpopular and for one reason or another the project misfired. It was everybody's business and nobody's business, Fuller commented, and, 'those children will have thin chaps and lean cheeks who have everybody (and yet nobody) nurses unto them'. Moreover it was a time when all sorts of schemes for overseas adventures were on foot and only those were rich who knew how to keep hold of their money: 'the world swarmed with prowling projectors.' King James had increasingly little money to spare as the reign advanced and Chelsea College developed no further than 'a lodge in a garden of cucumbers'. Years later, on the same site, King Charles II erected his hospital for old and disabled soldiers, and through the centuries the Chelsea pensioners have meditated on passed campaigns, as usefully may be and certainly as happily as black-coated divines would have meditated on the sins of Rome.

In so far as he shared in the lack of enthusiasm over the Chelsea scheme (and he certainly held up one church collection in his diocese so that his clergy would not be troubled with it till Easter and May-day were over, 'to the end the collection may be less grievous'), Andrewes may have been conscious of distaste for the continuance of controversy with Rome. With every year he felt more deeply the need of stressing the unity of Christendom and the simplicity of the fundamentals of Faith. Abbot, on the other hand, was something of a martinet in matters of theology and soon after he became Archbishop a tragic event took place for which he must take a large measure of the blame. On March 12th, 1612, Bartholomew Legate, the Arian, was burnt at Smithfield as a heretic and a month later a crazy Antinomian named Wightman suffered the same fate at Lichfield.

Bartholomew Legate was a young cloth-merchant who, after years of spiritual torment, had convinced himself that the true faith was not embodied in the Nicene and Athanasian Creeds and, as he put it in an earnest effort to explain, that Jesus Christ 'was a mere man as were Peter, Paul or I, only borne free from sinne'. This was blasphemy indeed, made worse rather than better by the fact that Legate was a young man of unblameable character, for, in Fuller's words, 'the poison of heretical doctrine is never more dangerous than when served up in clean cups and washed dishes'. The King and Archbishop were horrified and alarmed and Legate and his brother were brought before the Consistory Court of the Bishop of London, and upon their refusal to retract, were committed to Newgate.

James could not believe that if he himself, the anointed King, spoke to the obdurate cloth-merchant he would fail to convert him, and Legate was summoned to court. In a genuine attempt to save him despite himself, the King suggested that surely in his prayer Legate invoked the name of Christ. Legate answered that he had not done so for the past seven years, whereupon, with one of those sudden accesses of rage, James 'spurned at him with his foot', exclaiming 'it shall never be said one stayeth in my presence that has never prayed to our Saviour for seven years together'. Legate returned to prison, but upon the death of his brother soon afterwards he was released.

Just at this time the King's zeal for orthodoxy was stimulated. During one of his hunting expeditions he had been reading a book by the Dutchman, Vorstius, whose views of the nature of God were, James considered, 'monstrous opinions fitter to be remanded to Hell than committed to writing'. The King had communicated at once with his Ambassador at the Hague, bidding him inform the Dutch authorities how displeased he would be if Vorstius received any advancement in their Church. None the less Vorstius had been made Professor of Divinity at Leyden. The royal reputation as a theologian had been slighted; James was deeply hurt, and it was at this juncture that the unfortunate Legate threatened to sue the bishops for illegal imprisonment, thus drawing attention to himself just when the King was burning to impress the world as a champion of orthodoxy.

Once again Legate was taken into custody and brought a second time before the Consistory Court on February 21st, 1612. The personnel of the Court had been strengthened by the inclusion of three more bishops, Andrewes of Ely, Neile of Lichfield and Buckeridge of Rochester. Of Legate's heretical opinions there could be no question, and one cannot see, once the charge was preferred, how the Court could do other than convict him of heresy, even if the adjectives of ' obdurate, contumacious and incorrigible ', with which they branded him, were not exactly charitable. It was, however, this temper of Legate's mind, this very obdurateness, which made it impossible to hope for his conversion and there is no indication of any hesitance on the part of the judges in taking the final and painful step of ordaining that ' as a corrupt member ' he should be ' cut off from the Church of Christ and society of the faithful by the process of excommunication '. He was thereupon handed over to the secular arm for punishment.

There were certain legal doubts about the next step. That staunch upholder of the common law, Sir Edward Coke, doubted whether there were any laws extant to warrant the burning of heretics. But the King declared that if Legate were ' so desperate to deny Christ to be God ' he would adventure to burn him with a good conscience. He ordered his chancery to issue writs *de haeretico comburendi*, and on March 18th, 1612, the flames at Smithfield were lit again, and for the last time. Legate died unwavering to the end, ' and never did a scare-fire at midnight summon more hands to quench it than this at noonday did eyes to behold it '. Chamberlain reported the event without any grave concern; Legate, he commented earlier, had been ' long forborne and mildly dealt withall '; theoretically the action was justifiable according to the ethics of the time. But it was a different thing to see the victim die.

Those who watched, watched with a deep distaste. Whatever the dangers of heresy this was no way to stifle it. A month later, when Wightman perished at Lichfield, the men of the Midlands echoed the verdict of the Londoners. ' Indeed,' Fuller continues, ' such burnings of heretics much startled common people, pitying all in pain and prone to asperse justice itself with cruelty because of the novelty and hideousness of the punishment.'

One does indeed wish that Andrewes had voiced with the tones of authority the right feeling of the common people and left us with some evidence that he deplored the terrible thing that had occurred. There is no indication that he advised the King in the matter and, in so far as James was guided by his bishops, it was Abbot whose orthodoxy had demanded a victim. Andrewes may have been present at Legate's first interview with the King, but there is no record of his feelings as to the eventual outcome. He did, however, make one reference to it in his letters to Cardinal Perron, where he mentions the fact that two heretics had recently been burnt in England to controvert the criticism that the Anglican compromise inevitably led to slackness in dogma and thence to heresy. There can be little doubt that, whatever his emotional reactions, intellectually Andrewes approved the extirpation of heresy, much as a bishop of to-day might agree to capital punishment and for much the same reason, the safety of the rest of the community.

Whatever his reactions to Legate's execution, it would of course be futile to attribute to Andrewes any modern ideas on the question of freedom of thought. He was, like most of his contemporaries, unaware that any such question existed. Chillingworth had to suffer the impact of doubt and the spiritual turmoil of conversion and reconversion, Jeremy Taylor had to see his Church in ruins and his sovereign slain, before they proclaimed their faith in this dangerous idea of freedom. It is true that a Baptist congregation in Bermondsey, which had come into being in this same crucial year of 1612, justified its very existence by its belief in man's right to choose his own way to salvation. Already in politics, in religion, in economics those forces had been set in motion which, before the century was out, would usher in the age of toleration. But that tolerance was in part at least made possible by the gradual elimination of fear, and only to-day, when fear has again sharpened our perceptions, do we realize once again the price that must be paid for freedom. In 1612 the conviction was shared by Andrewes and all save a few extremists that truth was absolute, and that infidelity in matters of belief led inevitably to infidelity in action. Casaubon came from Paris still shocked by the assassination of Henri Quatre; Andrewes never got over his horror at the intended slaughter of November 5th. These excesses, they believed, were due to wrong thinking, to a false belief in combating which they sacrificed to controversy talents that had been dedicated to learning. Other false beliefs of an Anabaptist variety had produced in Germany the excesses of the peasants' revolt in the previous century. Hence the justification for uniformity over non-essentials. As Andrewes put it in a typical sermon, 'after contention came schism, and after schism heresy! Satan seems somewhat shame-faced at first, asks but some small trifle. Give him but that he will be ready for greater points. If he win ground in the ceremonies then have at the Sacrament; if he can disgrace the one it will not be long but ye shall hear of him at the other.' Inconformity in worship and belief, practices and doctrines not upheld by the firm scaffolding of the Christian Faith, might lead, did lead, he honestly believed, to further excesses which ended no man knew where, in reverberations and explosions compared with which the Gunpowder Plot might come to resemble nothing more drastic than a squib in a child's play.

As for King James, there was in his make-up conflicting impulses, unresolved tensions that made it then, as ever since, impossible to get the measure of the man. The setting of violence which encircled his youth had given to his conscious self a desire for tranquillity, an ambition to impose by the force of persuasion, peace upon a disordered world. But beneath there was in him a sadistic twist, a petulant cruelty that hunted down witches, that burned Legate and sent Raleigh to the block. It was with no sense of incongruity that he let his victims perish to score a debating point in the dispute with Rome or to win over Spain to more amicable relations. He was too deeply engaged in grandiose schemes to recall that in the vision of the psalmist 'mercy and peace hath kissed each other'. Yet even he, after Legate's death, felt that something had gone awry. Another convicted Arian in Newgate was left there unmolested and though the fight for freedom of conscience had as yet only begun, the fires at Smithfield were not lit again.

VI

THE ESSEX DIVORCE
1612–18

THE SUNSET YEARS before 1612 that seem in retrospect a postscript to the great age of Elizabethan England seemed to the people of the time to mark a new beginning. Their quality of hopefulness was engendered less by James himself or the fortuitous chance of a new century than by the presence in England of the royal children growing in stature and accomplishment and pledges of a happy and prosperous future. Whatever the King lacked that Queen Elizabeth possessed to bind the people to him in love and loyalty, he had this great asset, a son to carry on the dynasty and one who was well-beloved and wise beyond his years. In 1612, Henry, Prince of Wales, was eighteen years of age, good to look at, well graced in all the accomplishments of youth, a lover of sea and ships, and an enthusiastic Protestant. He went often to the Tower to visit Raleigh, heard with interest of the progress of his History of the World, and did his utmost to secure his release. He did not agree overwell with his father and regarded with mixed feelings the latter's plan to reconcile Europe by marrying him to a Spanish princess and his sister to a Protestant German princeling. Indeed, he would have nothing to do with James' plan for a Spanish alliance, declaring roundly that those of differing religions did not make good bed-fellows. James had to postpone this part of his project till Charles, his second son, grew to marriageable age. But Henry was enthusiastic about the negotiations on foot for the betrothal of his sister Elizabeth to Frederick, the Count Palatine. Unhappily, before they were completed in the spring of 1612, the growing sense of security received a shock in the death of Robert Cecil, Earl of Salisbury. As the King's first minister he had formed a link between the old régime and the new, and when he died, worn out in his country's service, to which he had sacrificed domestic comfort and the fruits of leisure, he left no effective successor in the task of government. The Howards, as greedy as they were ambitious, were left in triumphant prominence, and only the Prince of Wales' entourage could focus the opposition already stirring against them.

The negotiations with the Palatinate were successfully concluded and in the autumn of 1612 Frederick came to England to claim his betrothed. Already there were rumours abroad that the Prince of Wales was unwell; he had eaten immoderately of fresh fruit and had caught a chill playing games with too much vigour in the heat. In October he rallied, but only to succumb to a further attack of what has since been diagnosed as typhoid fever. The absence of the King and Queen from Whitehall, when Andrewes preached the customary sermon on November 5th, was the first sign to many that things were seriously wrong. On November 6th, Prince Henry died, with a cry on his lips for his sister who had been kept away for fear of infection and had tried in vain to get past the guards in disguise. It was a broken-hearted Princess who stood, a month later, by the side of the young German she was to marry, while Thomas Lake, one of Salisbury's former secretaries, read the betrothal articles in atrocious Latin.

On the Christmas day that followed the Prince's death, Bishop Andrewes preached as usual at Whitehall. The King, the Princess and young Prince Charles were present to hear his sermon, but there was no mention in it of the loss that had plunged the court in mourning. Yet it was perhaps the near presence of death which made him on this occasion focus his hearers' thoughts on Christ the great Healer, one who gave the medicine and was Himself the medicine ever present by the patient's couch. The Princess as she listened may have been comforted by the reminder that, after all, her brother had not been alone. In February she was married and the mixture of black and silver that she wore was a fitting symbol of the grief and hope with which she said farewell to her youth and pledged herself to a future of penury and exile and love. As the spring was blossoming on every hand she sailed away from the shores that she was not to see again for close on fifty years, years of hardship and adventure for herself and her children, years of tragedy and civil war for England.

The cleavage between crown and people, which did much to bring about that tragic conflict, was carried a stage further in the summer after the Princess's departure by certain events at court in which, unhappily, Andrewes was implicated. The Howards were now dominant at Whitehall. In 1613 the headship of that ancient Catholic family of wide estates and chequered loyalty was divided between the Lord Admiral Nottingham who, as Howard of Effingham, had defeated the Armada, and two other Earls, Northampton, clever, cultured and utterly unscrupulous, and Suffolk, an easy-going and not dishonest man cursed with a greedy and ill-tempered wife. Upon Salisbury's death the Treasury was put in commission with Northampton as first lord and his nephew Suffolk also on the board. They hoped to control the secretaryship by jockeying their protégé, Lake, into the vacant office, but the King refused to make any appointment, hoping to train as his secretary the young man upon whom his emotional life was centred, the Scottish favourite, Robert Carr, who had recently become Lord Rochester. Young Rochester had good looks and an easy temper, but neither brains nor strength of character, and James' attempt to instruct him in statecraft made it increasingly hard for him to pretend to an intelligence he did not possess. He saved himself by relying on the help and guidance of his friend Thomas Overbury, whose little book of *Characters*, published in 1610, showed him to be a man of considerable talent. Overbury was ambitious for Rochester and encouraged him to head a faction against the Howards, but the favourite had little taste for consistent intrigue and was too easy natured to wish to quarrel with anyone; besides, he had fallen in love with the Earl of Suffolk's youngest daughter.

Frances Howard had been married in her early teens to the young Earl of Essex, whom Andrewes had baptized in 1591 and who had grown up into an honest but rather uncouth young man. He had gone straight from his marriage to serve in the Netherlands, and when he returned to claim his bride in 1609, he found a spoilt young beauty, under the thumb of her greedy mother and the unscrupulous Northampton and deeply involved in a flirtation with Rochester. He bore her away protesting to his country home in Staffordshire, and for the next three years a strange and tragic farce was played out between them, in which Frances did everything in her power to prevent the consummation of her marriage. By interspersed moods of temper and frigidity, by every feminine wile that she could muster, and by the secret administration of drugs that she had obtained through the agency of a laundress, she succeeded in preserving herself for the man she loved from the man who was her husband.

The position was intolerable; early in 1613 the Howards approached Essex through his friend Southampton and it was mutually agreed to ask the King for an annulment of the marriage. James at once appointed a commission consisting of the Archbishop of Canterbury as chairman, four bishops, including Andrewes, and six lay members, four of whom were lawyers. They met in May, 1613, to consider the suit which Frances submitted.

Andrewes had no liking for the new assignment, and he showed his distaste for the whole affair by an obstinate silence which nettled Archbishop Abbot. He had hoped that Andrewes' knowledge of Canon law would enable him to unearth some instance which would clarify the legal position. After three years' co-habitation a suit for nullity could be granted and the commission's task might not have been unduly difficult but for two disturbing factors; Essex's determined refusal to admit that he was impotent, save in the case of this one woman, and Frances' known intention to marry Rochester the moment a divorce could be obtained. This fact, which made the King eager for the nullity and for the removal of any barrier which stood in the way of his favourite's happiness, made Abbot equally certain that he could not conscientiously agree to the divorce.

Another who opposed it was Overbury who was offered a post abroad in an effort to get him out of the way and upon his refusal committed to the Tower. As the summer wore on his parents were worried to hear that he was not well, but their enquiries went unheeded at Whitehall where all attention was centred on the divorce proceedings. His death before the autumn came passed almost unregarded.

The enquiry dragged on from May to September. Evidence was taken to prove the nullity of the marriage and the miserable years were traced out with no detail omitted to add verisimilitude to Frances' picture of herself as a docile wife cruelly tricked by fate. Abbot sought in vain for the key to what had really happened. Andrewes kept silent. To his sensitive spirit it was the wretched, unhappy hearts of this ill-mated pair that mattered; this cruel farce of three years' standing was a vicious caricature of Christian marriage; if legally permissible, it were surely right to end it. But Abbot was certain that something was wrong though he knew nothing of the intercourse between Frances and Mrs. Turner, the Hammersmith laundress who supplied the court with a fashionable yellow starch and dealt in drugs as a side line. Essex's reply to the suit cleared up nothing and even after Frances had been examined by a committee of matrons and seven kinswoman had testified to the truth of her deposition, Abbot was still unconvinced and the commissioners waited on the King at Windsor to inform him that they could not agree.

Andrewes had not as yet made his own attitude clear but at Windsor the King had a serious talk with him which, according to Abbot, influenced Andrewes' subsequent action. 'My lord of Ely,' he wrote, 'for a great while was in dislike of

the separation (as I have credibly heard he opened himself to
Sir H. Savile) until such time as the King spake with him
and then his judgment was reformed. But truth is that
amongst us, he said nothing.' Abbot himself found no enlightenment at Windsor, and when the commission next met
he voiced his objections to the divorce, not by a frank statement of his suspicions of collusion or foul play, but in a rather
ineffective speech full of scriptural allusions. 'My lord of
Ely sat little less than dumb.' All day the argument went
hither and thither and in the evening someone suggested another attempt at reconciliation. And then, unexpectedly,
Andrewes '. . . spake home about that, much disliking that
any such thing should now be sought; that it was too late; that
it might be the cause of poisoning and destroying one or another, to bring them together again'. Here, as far as he was
concerned, was the root of the matter. He had few illusions
about Frances' character and saw that she walked the razor's
edge of desperation; he had certainly no wish to argue the
matter further, it seemed to him a matter of broken hearts
rather than Canon law. He knew how the King felt about
things, the King whose judgment he respected and who spoke,
he believed, with divine authority. Knowing nothing of the
means whereby Frances had preserved her virginity, believing
that the evidence, if true—and it had been given on oath—
justified a suit for nullity, ignorant like the rest of the world
of all the lurid truth the years were to reveal, it seemed to
Andrewes that divorce was the most Christian way out of a
cruel tangle, the only decision that might give back to Essex
a chance of normal human happiness and open up for Frances
a way of regeneration.

The King ordered the commission to meet again in September after the summer break, and Andrewes went down as
usual to his diocese. He called on Abbot before he left London, and spoke of the weather and the danger of floods in the
Isle of Ely, but not a word of the nullity. Nor is there any
indication in his letters or writings that he was unduly troubled
by the affair, though when he found on his return that James

had added two more bishops to the commission, who would vote the way the King wished, he seems to have thought he need no longer attend. But, according to Abbot, James sent Andrewes a special request to be present when sentence was given, and he duly complied. On September 25th the commission declared that the divorce should be granted and the parties be at liberty to marry again. Archbishop Abbot and Bishop King of London were absent; Andrewes and the other bishops assented. However he may have erred in judgment or regretted in later years the step he took, Andrewes, who was always his own most severe critic, must have believed that the decision was one that he could make in all honesty. For in pronouncing judgment the commissioners first invoked the name of Christ, ' setting God before [their] eyes', and no pressure from the King or any other source, no weight of evidence or fear of future calamity would have caused Andrewes to commit sacrilege by using such a phrase and voting against his conscience. That evidence is incontrovertible.

At Christmas, Rochester and Frances were married and all Whitehall shared in the festivities. The students of the Inns of Court produced a masque, written by Bacon, and John Donne wrote a congratulatory ode. Even Sir Ralph Winwood, a man of severe integrity, made the bride a present of his famous black horses. But Archbishop Abbot continued to stand aloof.

Rochester was created Earl of Somerset and for a while the King was as happy as he had hoped to be. But Somerset was so devoted a husband that he neglected the King! There were undignified scenes and recriminations and on a visit to Apthorpe in 1614, James was first introduced to a beautiful young man called George Villiers. Villiers soon came to court and was groomed for the role of favourite by those who hated the Howards. And then fate struck. A one-time apothecary's boy, dying at Flushing, confessed to the murder of Overbury. James, inexpressibly shocked, ordered an immediate enquiry, and before long the whole sordid truth was

out; of Frances' use of Mrs. Turner the laundress, of tarts and
other food conveyed into the Tower by Overbury's keeper,
and of the Warden's accidental discovery and unhappy collusion. All these lesser men were taken, condemned and
executed. In his extremity the Warden's wife asked that
Andrewes might visit him as the only person to whom he was
likely to tell the truth. In the spring of 1616 Frances and her
husband stood their trial and were found guilty. The King
spared their lives; Somerset had a place in his heart that no
other could ever fill. But it was mistaken clemency and not
only because it cast aspersions on the royal justice; the unhappy
couple, when at length they were released, lived on in
wretchedness, hating where once they had loved, and seeing
in each other the living agent whereby their souls had been
destroyed.

It was against this background of greed and intrigue and
vice that Lancelot Andrewes pursued his tranquil way. These
were the years of his prominence at court with an unrivalled
reputation as a scholar and a preacher. 'An excellent sermon
by the Bishop of Ely' was as integral to the scene on great
occasions as were the masques and valentines or those yellow
ruffs that were so fashionable before the discovery of the in-
famous doings of Mrs. Turner. The question remains how
to reconcile these sermons and 'the sweet fragrance of his
name' with the temper of his surroundings and the character
of his associates.

The answer lies perhaps in his qualities of charity and single-
mindedness. As he went quietly about his business, keeping
himself aloof from political entanglements, concentrating as
far as possible on matters connected with the Church or
scholarship, his 'hazel eyes, very shrewd and untroubled'[1]
looked out on the life of London and the court with a clarity
of vision not possible to men and women emotionally tur-
moiled. He saw the sins and strivings of himself and his
fellows against the blinding glory of the presence of God.
Against that background all men were sinners, the best as the

[1] David Mathew, *The Jacobean Age*, p. 77.

worst, yet all through Christ might be saved. It was his task to show them the way of salvation and he did so in his intense humility as one whose need was as great as theirs. Every day in his prayers he abased himself, less through a consciousness of error in this matter or in that, as through a sense of his own utter unworthiness as he pondered the divine love. Another of sterner mould might have rebuked more firmly the sins of his contemporaries. He was content to pray for them as for himself and to pray with deep compassion. Having done so, he went out from his closet to the duties and pleasures of the life to which he had been called, ready to act with vigour but in charity and in the quiet confidence of one whose mind is stayed on God. This was the secret alike of his detachment and of his influence, for he left upon men a sense of abiding goodness, to which they responded as men always will to goodness rooted in humility and love.

VII

THE PREACHER

'THE BISHOP OF ELY preached at court on Christmas Day with great applause', Chamberlain reported in 1609, 'being not only "*sui similis*" but more than himself by the report of the King and all his auditors.' Indeed, the King had been so moved himself that he had asked for Andrewes' notes to lay them under his pillow. Ten years later in the March of 1620 Chamberlain was still reporting his friend's excellent preaching, 'and there was the greatest throng', he noted, 'that ever I saw at a sermon'. For more than thirty years in this manner Andrewes influenced the people of his day. Yet the sermons are strangely lacking in any reference to those public events of which they were the accompaniment. The Bishop conceived it to be his task not to direct men as to their duty in this political crisis or that social predicament, but to summon them back steadily and relentlessly to the contemplation of the eternal verities. The men of the Tudor and Stuart ages never entirely forgot the impact of eternity and alongside the cruelty and rapacity of the age, even in the moral stagnation of James' court, there went a spiritual awareness which made it possible for witch hunts and the authorized version, Bacon's bribes and his *Advancement of Learning*, Andrewes' *Devotions* and his adulation of the King, to exist together in mutual incompatibility. Such contrasts there always are and always must be, while man is a sinner and yet made in God's own image, but seldom can they have been so strongly marked as in the decades when Andrewes' sermons invoked a genuine

74

and enthusiastic response from a court where murder and adultery, corruption and greed were rampant. Across the grandeur and futility, the selfish scheming and the empty love affairs of the Palace of Whitehall the Bishop's words fell like the clear, cool notes of a bell calling the world to prayer.

He did not lift up his listeners on great waves of oratory or stir their hearts with uneasy emotion, as John Donne, tormented mystic, played upon the feelings of those who heard him. In the immediate future, when the theological treatises of Puritan divines and the balanced phrases of Latitudinarian bishops had changed the taste in sermons, his reputation suffered for a while, but to the age of Shakespeare and the Euphuists, as to-day to T. S. Eliot, Andrewes' respect for words made an immediate appeal, while his burning sincerity, the liveliness of his attack and deep tenderness of feeling give the sermons value for every age.

Not for him novelty or debate; sufficient one of the familiar texts suitable to the season, Lent or Passiontide or Christmas. Seventeen sermons on the Nativity, preached between the years 1605 and 1621, serve well to illustrate the method and spirit of his approach. The doctrine of the Incarnation would serve for 17 or 17,000 sermons; he need not deviate from his subject, relevant to every aspect of life. He began by dissecting his text as a scholar and a linguist. Those vacations in London, always studying some new language, had not been without effect on his mental processes; he could take a word and shake it, like a dog with a bone, basing an argument on an *ecce* or a *cum* till the pedagogue King and his sophisticated court marvelled anew at the unexpected treasures he revealed. It was a method that might be abused, and a Scot, who heard him on the northern journey in 1617, complained ' [he] takes up a thing and tosses and plays with it and then he takes up another and plays a little with it. Here's a pretty thing and here's a pretty thing '. But more often than not this juggling with moods and tenses led up to a vigorous spiritual appeal. At the very moment when the assembly of words might seem nought but dry bones, the wind of the

spirit blew, and the scholar became the saint, speaking simply
and directly to the hearts of his hearers and making them
marvel as never before at the thought of God incarnate, 'a
little child's flesh, not a span long', 'a stable for His cradle,
poor clouts for His array'. 'We blame them that this day
received Him in a stable; take heed we do not worse ourselves,' he added, or reminded them of their own need of a
Saviour. 'And for that, men may talk what they will, but
sure there is no joy in the world to the joy of a man saved.
. . . In danger of perishing by sickness, to hear of one will
make him well again; by sentence of the law, of one with a
pardon to save his life; by enemies, of one that will rescue and
set him in safety. . . . And it may be, we need not any of
these; we are not presently sick, in no fear of the law, in no
danger of enemies. . . . But that which He came for, that
saving we need all; and none but He can help us to it.'

Simplicity and a wide sympathy were the hall-marks of
Lancelot Andrewes' goodness; his erudition might mask but
it could not destroy the painstaking and honest kindliness that
was in part an heritage of his merchant-seaman parentage.
The unnecessary complications which men brought into their
lives by their political ambitions, their theological disputes,
their passion for property bred in him a deep pity for the
foolishness of mankind, who should have been joyful with the
'fulness of joy'. It was in 1609, in the sermon that pleased
the King so much, that he hammered home the idea of fulness,
an idea that meant much to him in his appreciation of the
riches and beauty of the created universe. In the succeeding
year he spoke of 'joy', and this thrusting upon the attention
of one word or one idea by emphasis and reiteration and
diverse interpretation was characteristic of his method. He
would *compel* folk to hearken and to remember, and whatever
nuances they forgot, they would bear away one essential truth.

It was in 1622 when the shadows were lengthening alike for
him and for his royal master that he preached upon the text
'Behold there came wise men', and used in describing their
winter journey the words which T. S. Eliot has embodied in

the opening lines of his poem *The Magi*—'A cold coming they had of it.' He spoke of their wearisome, irksome, troublesome, dangerous, unseasonable journey and contrasted it with our own expectation of an easy approach to God. 'If rugged or uneven the way, the weather ill-disposed, if any never so little danger, it is enough to stay us.'

Yet come men must! Whether his text was from Isaiah or St. Luke, however many his quips and fancies as he unravelled his meaning, deep as was his sympathy with men's frailty, he knew, and in every sermon concluded with the reminder that the salvation offered by God did not reach men automatically. It required from them an effort of will, an eager response; as He had come to them, so they must also *come*. It was not sufficient to contemplate the mystery nor to rest in an assurance of grace; man must act. And the action must be twofold, in work and worship, in humility and fruitfulness. The trouble with the average man, Andrewes sadly commented, was his readiness to be puffed up by any victory in the realms of virtue: 'if we happen to be anything fruitful . . . straight we cease to be little; we begin to talk of merit and worth and I wot not what'. And immediately the good work became worthless, for 'humility is the first comma of the sentence where eternity is the period'. The good fruit which sprang from a life rooted in faith and obedience was part of the worship man owed to God, for worship was far more than silent communing between a man and his maker, it was the offering of the whole self, soul and body and possessions. And it reached its supreme expression in the Sacrament, which gave to every man a chance to come with the Magi and the shepherds into Christ's own presence, to receive from Him strength to be led more surely in the Way. Here every sermon ended as the words of man fell silent before the Word.

It is perhaps in the sermons on the Nativity that a reader of to-day will find most that is helpful and congenial. But there are many lovely passages to be found in the other sermons, particularly in those preached on Whit Sunday. It was in one of these that Andrewes pleaded so urgently for unity and accord in men's individual souls as in the life of community. At Holyrood House in 1617 his text was from St. Luke, 'The Spirit of the Lord is upon me because He hath anointed me that I should preach the Gospel to the poor . . .' and he spoke of Christ's commission to 'cure the broken hearts and release the prisoners' with the tenderness that he always bore towards ordinary folk and people in distress. He referred to the poor. '. . . They are not troubled with much worldly good news; seldom come there any posts to them with such. But the good news of the Gospel reacheth even the meanest.' He spoke of those most truly captives, 'held in slavery to sin and Satan', and declared that only the 'broken-hearted' could hope to hear the word of God, broken if not by a worldly cross, then by the sight of their own sins. 'And this be sure if a man be not humbled with the sight of his sins, it is not all the crosses or losses in the world will humble him aright. But if we run away from our own hearts, be ever abroad, never within, God must send some bodily sickness, some worldly affliction to send us home unto ourselves. But sure the Angel must come down and the water be stirred, else we may preach long enough to uncontrite hearts, but no good will be done till then. Then it will be possible to proclaim the good news of redemption and restitution, of the acceptable year.'

A large part of the sermon dealt with the working of the Holy Spirit, which Andrewes compared to an anointing. 'An ointment is a composition we know; the ingredients of it oil and sweet odours. By virtue of the oil it soaks even into the bones, saith the Psalm; but it works upon the joints and sinews sensibly, making them supple and lithe, and so the more fresh and active to bestir themselves. By virtue of the sweet odours mixed with it, it works upon the spirits and senses; cheers him and makes him " glad " that is anointed with it. And not him alone, but all that are about and near him . . . that take delight in his company, to go and to run with him, and all for the fragrant sweet scent they feel to come from him.'

Was it just chance that so many in speaking of Andrewes use this very analogy of fragrance? 'The ointment of whose

name is sweeter than all spices,' Hacket wrote of him. There
are other passages typical of Andrewes in the sermon. The
scholar appears in his stress on the need to 'light our lamps
oft and to spend much oil on our studies that we may strike
off and gather safely this precious ointment that "lieth thick"'
on the pages of the Scriptures and the Christian Fathers.
Typical also is that description of the 'joints and sinews' made
'the more fresh and active to bestir themselves'. For
Andrewes' goodness was never merely that of the scholar or
recluse; he makes the point on another occasion that goodness
is a positive virtue, not merely the absence of wrongdoing.
His gentleness can be overstressed if it gives the impression
of a languid spirit; it was the energy as well as the love of
God which inspired him. It was, for instance, the effectiveness of his almsgiving that always struck his contemporaries,
and the practical help he was always ready to give to individuals in distress was the disciplined compassion of one who had
trained himself to understand men's needs and to assist them
with the vigour as well as sympathy of one who always kept
his joints and sinews 'fresh and active'. 'He wholly spent
himself,' said Buckeridge in the funeral sermon, 'as if he
had minded nothing else all his life long but this, to offer himself, his soul and body, a contrite and a broken heart, a pitiful
and compassionate heart, and a thankful and grateful heart, a
living sacrifice, holy and acceptable to God.'

Lancelot Andrewes was a master of his art, and from the
printed page, three centuries gone by, one cannot hope to catch
the full flavour of his preaching. He tried not to bore his congregation, to judge by one of his comments: 'For this we
find, that while one goes on still with a tale in a continued
tenour of speech, attention grows dull, and no readier way to
awake it . . . than suddenly to break off the point we were in
hand with and turn to quite another matter, which with the
strangeness will affect the hearer, and make him listen afresh,
whether he will or no.' He had no exaggerated ideas about
the value of preaching; his steady practice of prayer combined
with his reliance upon the sacraments to give him a sure sense

of proportion in this matter. It was, however, one about which
there was a certain divergence of opinion. The prophesyings
of Elizabeth's reign and Reynolds' insistence at Hampton
Court that the dearth of good preachers was a serious blemish
in the Church, illustrate the importance the Puritans attached
to sermons, whereby the learned and devout might instruct
their congregations in a proper interpretation of the Scriptures.
Men of Bancroft's type feared an over-emphasis at the expense
of worship, and Andrewes did in the sermon at Holyrood refer
to the dangers of going beyond one's text. But on the question
as a whole he was, as always, in favour of harmony and good
sense. '[It is] folly,' he declared, 'to fall into comparisons,
to set them [prayer and preaching] at odds together, these two
ways, as the fond fashion nowadays is. Make use of both. It
may be, who knows, if the one will not work, the other may.'
In that faith he went steadily on, never losing hope for his
fellow men, praying for them in his private devotions and in
the ordered worship of every day, and preaching to them on
every great festival, without ever losing a sense of the reality
and the urgency of his message. So at the centre of the
changing life of his time, there stood the crowded chapel of
Whitehall, and there one can imagine the court in all its glory
of array, the keen intellects sharpened on Elizabethan wit, the
torn hearts of such as Frances Howard, the soiled hands of
Lord Chancellor Bacon, Salisbury worn out and on the verge
of death, Queen Anne weeping at a reference to her dead son,
and in the pulpit the serene, shrewd old man, illuminating with
a scholar's skill the precious words of the gospel, stressing with
sudden sternness their own poverty and wretchedness, tenderly
showing them the simplicity and peacefulness of the good life,
and without hesitation, as the shepherd of his flock, leaving
them at the end where they should be, at the Altar of the living
God, eager for the gift of His very Self that alone could heal
their infirmities and preserve them in body and soul.

In the latter years of James' reign a new star appeared in
the ecclesiastical firmament and John Donne's preaching came
to equal or even surpass that of the ageing Bishop Andrewes.

In March 1617 Archbishop Abbot and Mr. Secretary Winwood went to Paul's Cross to hear Donne preach and the news-writer reported that he 'was exceedingly well-liked generally, the rather that he did Queen Elizabeth great right and held himself close to the text without flattering the time too much'. Donne had less depth of scholarship than Andrewes, but a personal devotion to St. Augustine and a respect for Aquinas that rooted him securely in medieval culture in spite of an eagerness of mind in touch with new patterns of thought. His spiritual life was enriched with a poetic mysticism that Andrewes entirely lacked, an emotional awareness for which a price had to be paid. Not for Donne the tranquil and natural growth into Christian manhood that had been Andrewes' happy lot. His whole life had been a struggle, a paradox. In childhood his parents' loyalty to the Roman Catholic religion made him familiar with hardship and sudden death. As a young man, he visited Italy and sailed under Essex's flag, but neither adventure nor love affairs brought him satisfaction, as he sought feverishly for the elixir of life in the shifting sands of experience.

In 1601, after four years of respectable calm as Secretary to Lord-Keeper Egerton, Donne disgraced himself by a secret marriage with Ann More, Lady Egerton's favourite niece, and until the angry father relented, eight years later, and paid his daughter's dowry, they lived a penurious life in a damp and draughty house at Mitcham. Donne was only saved from bitterness of spirit and actual want by the help of a Yorkshire clergyman, Thomas Morton. Morton, who later became Bishop of Chester, was then engaged on a theological work in which he asked Donne's assistance, but even more valuable than this financial aid was the invigorating influence of his own stability and kindness of heart. For Morton, slight, spruce and practical, was above all a man of good courage. In his early days in York he had refused to be daunted by the Plague and had ridden round the stricken streets of the city distributing food from his saddle-bag, and in his old age, during the Commonwealth, he maintained 'even at his lowest ebb a cheerful heart and a decent appearance'. His friendship for Donne enabled the latter to win through to peace of mind and, eventually, though not till 1615, to agree to be ordained. Thereafter his reputation grew rapidly. In 1621 he became Dean of St. Paul's and stepped almost at once into the position Andrewes could no longer fill. Izaak Walton has left us a picture of Donne, in these years of fruition, one of God's saints in his deepening love and faith, more subtle, more emotional than Andrewes could ever be, appealing to the heart rather than the head, to the poetry of words rather than their derivation, but with the same deepening sense of personal communion with God. In an age when so much was awry, so much in flux, these two jewels of the English Church shone with a greater brightness by reason of the vulgarity and corruption of so much of their surroundings, the one a scholar, the other a poet, so different in their mentality and their background, but both finding within the framework of the Anglican communion a spiritual home in their pilgrimage on earth.

VIII

FRIENDSHIPS

IT CAN seldom have been more pleasant to be a scholar in England than in the years of transitory prosperity that preceded the rash acceptance by the King's son-in-law of the crown of Bohemia in 1618. The stresses and strains of the Reformation and of the fervent nationalism of the Elizabethan era had mellowed into a seeming harmony between Church and State, prince and prelates, and the purlieus of Whitehall was a fruitful field for the alumni of Oxford and Cambridge, sunning themselves in the patronage of a King who loved learning. They all knew each other; if they had not been to school together at Westminster or St. Paul's or Merchant-Taylors, they had been undergraduates at Trinity or Balliol, Peterhouse or Christ's, and shared an interest in theology or the fine arts or the new experimental science.

Bacon, writing his *Advancement of Learning* and planning the greater work which should revolutionize man's whole conception of the natural world, looked for support both to grandees like the sophisticated Northampton and to prelates such as Bancroft. On his list of likely patrons appeared the name of Lancelot Andrewes, who was stated to be not only rich and single and therefore likely to have money to spare for the furtherance of scientific learning, but one who had already acted as kindly mentor in revising the *Advancement* and had indulged in a few experiments himself.

Lancelot Andrewes was a beloved and familiar figure at the very heart of this scholarly nexus in the London of his day.

He possessed to the full the characteristics of a good friend. Generous in spirit and gentle in temper, with a ready wit and a well-stored mind, his company was at once restful and stimulating. One could be sure in his home of domestic comfort, good conversation and spiritual refreshment. Moreover, he must have been in his prime a happy man; he liked the King; he believed whole-heartedly in the episcopacy to which he was proud to belong; he suffered no material hardships, and his hours of devotion gave him at all times a sense of the companionship of God.

There was a considerable amount of coming and going between England and the Continent in the decade that preceded the outbreak of the Thirty Years' War. Andrewes, with his fifteen languages and his European reputation, was one of those whom scholars from abroad made a point of visiting. It was in the autumn of 1610 that the arrival of the eminent classicist, Isaac Casaubon, brought him a new acquaintance who, during the next four years, came to mean much to him. Casaubon was a scholar whose only vice was buying books. Scion of an ancient Huguenot family, he had lived for many years in Geneva, eventually migrating to Paris, where he became royal librarian and rose high in the favour of Henri IV. He was particularly interested in the problems of the English Church, for he hankered after some such compromise, resisting all efforts to convert him to Catholicism but out of sympathy with the Calvinist theology of his Huguenot forebears. After the assassination of Henri IV he came over to England and was entertained in London by Overall, the Dean of St. Paul's, who introduced him to Andrewes to the mutual satisfaction of the two scholars. They soon found that metaphorically they ' talked the same language ', and that literally they could converse in Latin and French far more easily than Casaubon could with most of his new acquaintances, for English was a tongue he never learnt to master.

A few weeks later Casaubon was summoned to Theobald's to be presented to the King. It was James' delight at supper on a Sunday evening to indulge in debate with such learned men as could be mustered. As the King's Almoner, Andrewes was frequently in attendance, and his gift of silence stood him in good stead, for in effect the discourse often turned into a royal soliloquy! It was on one of these Sunday evenings that Casaubon was presented. He was in a mood of some trepidation. He was by nature a humble, sometimes a querulous, man, small in stature, often in physical discomfort, always short of money, and at the moment nostalgic for the wife and the books he had left behind in Paris. Perhaps his diffidence stood him in good stead. The King approved of him, and hereafter Casaubon gained most of his knowledge of the English countryside from hurried journeys on Sunday evenings to Greenwich or Windsor or wherever the court might be.

It was not long before his acquaintance with Andrewes ripened into intimate friendship. They shared the same academic interests and a like zeal for patristic learning and the more they talked the more they had in common. To his friends in Europe Casaubon wrote with enthusiasm. 'I am by way of seeing the bishop daily. I am attracted to the man by his profound learning, and charmed by a graciousness of manner, not common in one so highly placed.' And again '. . . we spend whole days in talk of literature—sacred especially—and no words can express what true piety, what uprightness of judgement I find in him'.

In the summer of 1611 Andrewes visited his diocese as usual and took Casaubon with him away from the infection of the London streets in August. They stayed the night in Cambridge at Peterhouse, and went on through the flat fen country to Downham. Casaubon remained for six or seven weeks and only much against Andrewes' will did he leave at length to get back to a colossal work on Church history, which his failing health made it increasingly hard to tackle. Andrewes invited him to stay again in 1612, but a foreboding that his time was short kept him at his books, though the Bishop tempted him with the coolness of the weather in the fen country, where he himself had even caught a chill, and offered him as alternative attractions a ' Hebrew St. Matthew ', which was in Corpus library, or a visit to Stourbridge Fair.

Casaubon only lived for two more years, not very happy ones, for he was always short of money and felt himself neglected as the novelty of his presence wore off. Overall, Morton and Andrewes remained his loyal friends, and in 1614 his eldest son, Meric, was confirmed by Andrewes and became a full member of the English Church. This gave the Bishop intense satisfaction; he was tremendously encouraged by the fact that Casaubon, working along independent lines, had reached the same conclusion as the English divines and envisaged as not only possible but needful a Church like their own, episcopal and sacramental in nature, based on the teaching of the Christian Fathers, but independent of Rome, and therefore free of the accretions in doctrine and ritual which the Roman Church had acquired during the Middle Ages. Casaubon's approval, so Andrewes felt, saved the English Church from insularity, and the stress he laid on its Catholicity in the best and fullest sense of the word accorded with Andrewes' own deepest conviction.

Casaubon died in July 1614. During the last few days Andrewes was constantly at his friend's bedside and, at the end, administered the sacrament and said the Nunc Dimittis, which the dying man repeated ' not without effort '. Andrewes sent to Heinsius, the Dutch scholar, an account of Casaubon's death, and wrote with feeling of one ' always devoted to the cause of truth and peace '. He was indeed a congenial spirit and his going left a blank in Andrewes' life that was never quite to be filled.

Among the Bishop's many other friends might be counted Dean Overall, who rejoiced, like himself, in the company of European scholars, had behind him a similar career of distinction at Cambridge, shared on the same committee in the labours of the translation, and above all looked at the Church from the same angle of vision. Overall was no preacher. He said himself that ' he had spoken Latin so long it was troublesome to him to speak English in a continued oration '. As prolocutor of the lower House of Convocation, he helped to draw up the Canons of 1604, and he added to the catechism the passage on the sacraments which contains that satisfying definition, 'the outward and visible sign of an inward and spiritual grace'.

Of his colleagues on the episcopal bench Neile and Buckeridge were Andrewes' closest associates. Neile, like himself, was the son of a London tradesman, though a tallow-chandler can scarcely have ranked so high as a master-mariner; Buckeridge had been at Merchant-Taylors, but fell from grace in Andrewes' eyes by going to the older university. Neile was a true Cockney; not very scholarly, for he said he had been flogged too much at Westminster ever to learn Latin, but with a ready wit and boundless energy and a measure of common-sense that saved him from extreme action in spite of his extreme opinions. His first bishopric was that of Rochester in 1608, where one of his chaplains was William Laud, whose close friend and ally he remained in the stormy years ahead. When Bishop of Durham in 1617, Neile made his episcopal residence in the Strand a centre of High Church influence and his enthusiasm and vigour, while it made him popular with court and clergy, gave him a less happy reputation with the parliament men as an excessive defender of the royal prerogative. In his equally lovely palace across the river, Andrewes, as Bishop of Winchester, lived out his conception of a great prelate, but said less about it. One tale is told of him and Neile which is characteristic. On one occasion when they were in attendance upon James, the King asked with some impatience if he might not take his subjects' money without all the fuss and formality of Parliament. Neile answered, 'God forbid, Sir, but you should, you are the breath of our nostrils.' Andrewes was quiet at first, but when he was pressed replied, 'Sir, I think it is lawful for you to take my brother Neile's money, because he offers it.'

Buckeridge was by temperament more congenial to Andrewes than was Neile. At St. John's College, Oxford, he had shown himself firm but unprovocative in his maintenance of the High Church point of view. He succeeded Andrewes at

St. Giles, Cripplegate, and shared something of his reputation as a preacher. 'A very pious, worthy and learned bishop,' said contemporary opinion. Buckeridge preached Andrewes' funeral sermon and spoke with feeling of their friendship: 'I loved and honoured him for above thirty years space.' It was he who published Andrewes' ninety-six sermons, with the help of Laud, that bundle of contradictions, who carried on Andrewes' work in the Church but failed so utterly to emulate his Christian serenity.

There were, however, many others besides bishops in Andrewes' circle of friends. Casaubon was only the first and most intimate of the scholars of European repute, of whom Grotius was the greatest, who accounted a meeting with Lancelot Andrewes as one of the attractions of an English visit. It is always to be remembered that he was a scholar as well as a divine, and that the basic shape and colouring of his thought remained that of a classicist and historian. It was this deep concern with the ancient world and with the historical processes whereby the England of his day had evolved which gave his theological thinking its own particular bias, and made him a fit person to be elected, as he was just before its closure, to the Society of Antiquaries. The growing influence of the lawyers in that society had roused the King's suspicions and early in James' reign it ceased to meet. Andrewes remained on friendly terms with many of its members, including Selden, and it is satisfactory to note that he approved the latter's controversial book on tithes as historically sound and therefore meritorious, however unpopular it might be with those who upheld the theory of divine right.

Another of his friends from the Society of Antiquaries was Thomas Bodley, a diplomat who loved books and who, in retirement, devoted his small fortune and his superabundant energy to restoring and re-stocking Duke Humphrey's ruined library at Oxford. In Bodley's letters to his librarian, Dr. James, there is a reference to a visit which Andrewes and Neile made to the new library and a rebuke for Dr. James because he had not reported all that they did and said. But the most distinguished of Andrewes' friends was undoubtedly the brilliant Francis Bacon. 'Amongst the men of our times, I hold you in special reverence,' Bacon wrote to Andrewes and in dedicating to him his fragmentary *Holy War* he refers to their 'ancient and private acquaintance', which dated from the time when Andrewes was at St. Giles and Bacon a student at the Inns of Court. When the latter sent a copy of *The Advancement of Learning* to his protégé Toby Matthew, who was travelling in Italy, he wrote: 'I thought it a small adventure to send you a copy, who have more right to it than any man, except Bishop Andrewes who was my inquisitor.' The reference is made clearer by a later letter from Bacon to Andrewes himself which accompanied the manuscript of the *Cogita et Visa,* a letter that begins with a half-serious reprimand: 'Nowe your lordship hath bene so longe in the Church and the Pallace disputing between Princes and Popes methinkes you should take pleasure to looke into the fields and refresh your minde with some matter of Philosophy.' Bacon asks his old Inquisitor to read through the manuscript and continues: 'Nowe lett mee tell you what my desire is. If your Lp. be soe good now as when you were the good deane of Westminster my request unto you is that not by pricks but by notes you would marke unto me, whatsoever shall seeme to you, either not currant in the stile, harsh to Creditt and opinion or inconvenient for the person of the Wrighter.' He had no intention of changing the main argument, he confessed. 'Yet even in those things the admonition of a friend may make me expresse myselfe diversly.' It was in this sort of intercourse that Andrewes found his deepest satisfaction, and it was indeed a tragedy that the next record of his association with Bacon, that intellectual giant whose moral sense had atrophied, was on the occasion of the latter's fall.

There was one friend whose ready pen has left us many glimpses of Andrewes and his circle. John Chamberlain, the news-writer, had been at Cambridge with Andrewes and was an acquaintance of long standing. Chamberlain had been, all his life, of delicate health and had left the university without taking a degree. But his father had endowed him with sufficient income for him to live in self-imposed retirement, half scholar, half man of the world, on easy terms with many of those who angled for favour in the purlieus of the court. He had few illusions about human nature, a clear and caustic way of expressing himself and a respect for the truth which enabled him in his news-letters to leave a good example of impartial reporting for the journalists of the future.

His first references to Andrewes belong to the earlier period in his friend's career, when the two men were still in fairly close touch. Chamberlain reported his friend's installation as Dean of Westminster, adding, 'Master Beeston and I supped with him in the hall among the electors'. He recorded his later preferments with friendly pride and interest, expressing indignation with Buckeridge when he thinks he has stolen some of Andrewes' ideas and obviously happy to be on terms of friendship with 'the good Bishop of Chichester'.

After his translation to Ely he still saw him fairly frequently, and when the Divorce case was pending, Chamberlain was one of the few people to whom Andrewes spoke of the matter. 'Ely,' Chamberlain wrote in August 1613, 'made no daintie to tell me his opinion which I could wish were otherwise if there be no more reason in it than I cld see or conceive.' There was a difference of opinion here that might well lead to a breach, but Andrewes saw to it that this did not occur. 'I have been lately twice or thrice with the Bishop of Ely,' Chamberlain reported in February 1614, 'who says he had sent after me ten or twelve times and now lastly would know whether I had left him.' And next year Andrewes and Winwood between them persuaded Chamberlain to put in an appearance when the court visited Cambridge, a particularly happy occasion for Andrewes who found that, in one of the formal debates on Philosophy staged for the King's benefit, four of the disputants were Pembroke men. He rewarded them with twenty angels apiece and felt that everything had gone exactly as it should.

Yet after this last pleasant meeting inevitably Andrewes and Chamberlain drifted apart. With every passing year the

Bishop's commitments grew; he was a man of affairs now as well as a scholar and a priest. Chamberlain, as sensitive as most men of delicate health, hesitated to approach him and was terrified of a snub. He watched from afar the factions at the court, multiplying now with such rapidity, as had been apparent in the ride to Windsor in May 1615 when two new Knights of the Garter vied with each other in the grandeur of his train. The one Lord Knollys, kinsman of the Cecils and the Howards, was backed by the great nobility, while Lord Fenton, a member of the Royal Household, could claim the support of the King's immediate servants and it is noteworthy that 'the Bishop of Ely sent eight men very well furnished and mounted, which led the Lord Fenton's troupe'. This was a different world from that in which Chamberlain had supped with the new Dean at Westminster, and next year their paths diverged still further. In October 1616 Chamberlain reported of him as a stranger: 'I had almost forgot that the Bishop of Ely was sworn of the Council on Michaelmas day which honour was done him to put him in heart upon the distaste he had in missing the bishopric of Winchester but for ought I hear he is yet as silent as Master Wake's nuntio, the new Cardinal.'

A year passed before Chamberlain met his old friend again. Then happily the breach was healed: 'I was very welcome to him and he used me with extraordinary kindness,' he reported. Immediately after he became Bishop of Winchester Andrewes invited him to dinner and now it was Chamberlain who could do his friend a good turn, for Andrewes was particularly interested in the Synod of Dort and asked if Carleton, who was now at the Hague, would send him a copy of the proceedings. 'He could make shift with the Dutch.'

So it continued during the remaining years of their lives, Chamberlain was still touchy at the least hint of neglect, but Andrewes still remembered to seek him out. He had him to dine on one occasion 'to take part of a stag the King had sent him the day before'. It must have been a good dinner for Selden was present, whose table-talk was inimitable, and of Andrewes himself Chamberlain wrote: 'I marvel every day more and more at the happiness of his memory for it seems that nothing escapes him of what he hath heard or read.' In spite of Chamberlain's testiness and Andrewes' multiplicity of engagements, riches and prosperity had not been able to divide them, and Chamberlain's admiration for his old acquaintance had stood the test of time.

IX

LATTER YEARS
1616–26

THE MIDDLE YEARS of King James' reign, undistinguished in politics or personalities, went their chequered way. The fall of the Somersets in 1615 was followed by the gradual eclipse of the Howards and the emergence of Villiers as the channel whereby all court favour flowed. Bacon, Privy Councillor in 1616, and eventually Lord Chancellor, grasped at the power after which he had always hankered only to find he had seized a bubble that burst in his hand and that real power still rested with the young man who had become Duke of Buckingham early in 1617.

Andrewes became a Privy Councillor at the same time as Bacon. He was resolutely determined to avoid faction and any share in those affairs of State which had no bearing upon the Church. He would ask on his arrival at the Council in the morning: 'Is there anything to be done to-day for the Church?' If the answer was no, he would be gone; if yes, he answered: 'I will stay.' He sat upon a certain number of royal commissions and spoke occasionally in the Star Chamber, as in Lady Rous' case when he justified the breaking of a vow if the refusal to do so impeded the course of justice. He was frequently engaged upon the work of the Court of High Commission, which was largely concerned at a higher level in the sort of moral surveillance which he also exercised through his diocesan visitations. His position as royal Almoner gave full

scope alike to his shrewdness and his generous impulses, and
there was no man living who gave such compassionate care to
the business of helping weaker brethren. These various commitments added to his episcopal duties and the preaching,
which he always considered his prime reason for being at
Whitehall, kept him more than adequately occupied.

There are two lines of a poem by one of Andrewes' young
friends that typify his approach alike to his secular and religious
duties.

> ' Who sweeps a room as for thy laws
> Makes that and the action fine '

wrote George Herbert, who had been a small boy at Westminster when Andrewes was Dean, and had later corresponded
with him as his ' Sanctissimus Pater ', when Herbert was at
Cambridge. The ethos of the Church they both loved so well
was made up of that very intermingling of soul and body,
inherent in a sacramental approach to life. In this faith they
both lived, and George Herbert achieved the unique position
he holds in the Anglican tradition not by any outstanding deed
of heroism or political wisdom but by virtue of a thin book of
verse and three years in a country village, fulfilling the ordinary
avocations of a parish priest and differing only from his fellows
in doing his job superlatively well.

For Lancelot Andrewes the way was not so plain as for
George Herbert. His own temperament, that of the scholar,
set against his special circumstances, those of the prelate-states-
man, introduced into his life a particular note of tension. In
Laud, that tension was to breed irritability, inconsistency,
strife; in Andrewes' case, his necessary preoccupation with
worldly affairs seems neither to have destroyed his own
serenity, nor lessened the regard in which he was held. His
deep desire for accord in church relationships was part and
parcel of the man, yet tragically he did less to further that
accord than he might have done. It was less timidity, though
even those who loved him wished he would speak out more

frequently, than an inability to understand the spiritual roots of Puritanism, which debarred him from that great work of reconciliation which might yet have been essayed. As it was, though he enriched his Church both in its worship and in its theology, he did not save it from the disharmony that was disrupting it, in spite of those many qualities of temper and intellect which made him so eminently suitable for the role of peacemaker.

In 1617 Andrewes accompanied the King on a journey to Scotland. James' visit was in part a sentimental journey, for it was his jubilee year, but he also wished to carry a stage further the establishment of episcopacy in Scotland, and to introduce into the worship of the northern kingdom such unpopular customs as the use of the cross and kneeling at the receipt of the Sacrament. To Andrewes these ceremonies were part of the ancient custom of the Church, and in the Easter sermon he preached at Durham he inveighed against 'such as had adulterate(d) the truth of God by devices of their own taking up, not with idolatry perhaps but, which is as evil and differs but a letter, with idealatry'. His whole objection to the innovations of would-be reformers was based on this conviction that the intrusion of individual whims and interpretations blurred men's apprehension of the fundamental gospel truths. He could not see that to some these ceremonies might be the very obstacles that stood in the way of the light.

Thanks largely to the wisdom and moderation of Archbishop Spottiswoode and the excellent Bishop Forbes of Aberdeen, the immediate results of James' visit satisfied him and, soon after their return home, Montague, the aged Bishop of Winchester, who had recently repaired and beautified his palace in South-wark, invited to the great feast, upon the completion of the work, 'all the Lords and others of quality that went the Scottish journey'. That was in November and either at this party or during the later Christmas festivities Andrewes was laid low with a sudden attack of indigestion that he put down to eating too much pork! He was unable to preach at court that Christmas and though in the new year he was up and about again, this was the first sign that he was not as young as he had been. Increasingly, he suffered from attacks of the stone and the gout, not improved by his dislike of dieting. In the autumn of 1618, upon Montague's death, he became Bishop of Winchester, and in the spring he moved across the river to Winchester House, the great palace on the Southwark side of the Thames. Next year, he gave up the post of royal Almoner but his appointment as Dean of the Chapel Royal maintained his close relationship with James, and for three years to come he continued to preach regularly at court. His country home was at Farnham where the King visited him twice, for it was excellent country for hunting and the Bishop entertained him magnificently. But Andrewes' own habits remained unchanged by wealth. He endeavoured increasingly to keep clear of political entanglements and to accustom himself to the contemplation of death. 'But now old age which of itself is a disease, and yet never cometh without diseases attending it, plucks me by the ear, and bids me get out of this cock-pit and rank myself with them, whose whole business is prayer.'

He wrote thus, in 1619, in the third of his letters to du Moulin the French Huguenot. Throughout this friendly exchange of views on the nature of episcopacy there is a gentle tone entirely different from the acerbities of the Bellarmine controversy. It shows Andrewes at his best. 'I have ever been both by nature and by choice addicted to peace,' he wrote, '. . . living under a King whose word is that of a saviour: "Blessed are the Peace-Makers."' After arguing the divine right of bishops, he concluded, 'though they be by Divine Right, we do not say these things belong to Faith'. And in a later letter, '. . . though our Government be by Divine Right, it follows not either that there is no salvation or that a Church cannot stand without it. He must needs be made of iron or hard-hearted that denies them salvation.' Though no man is clearer about his principles, there is in all Andrewes' judgments an awareness that rules may be overborne in the cause of Christian charity.

In the final letter to du Moulin Andrewes apologizes for a delay in writing. King James had been ill, he explained, struck down by a disease 'so intricate and doubtful that the physicians themselves were at a loss to stand what the event would be'. 'All I had to do,' Andrewes continues, 'was to fall to my prayers with many more who were sore perplexed, as then in jeopardy, for a most gracious King.' He goes on to reflect: 'He makes it not the least of his cares to tender the peace and order of his church here', and concludes: 'You yourself know (and indeed: who knows not since he hath wrote so much, so admirably?) that as he is most able in respect of his other endowments of wit and learning, so also in respect of his acuteness and solidity of judgment, he is equal to the best or rather goes before them.' Posterity has perhaps been too ready to dismiss James as the 'wisest fool in Christendom'; however many his faults, he gained and held the esteem of Lancelot Andrewes.

The King's recovery and the fact that the young Prince of Wales had now made friends with Buckingham lightened the atmosphere at Whitehall in 1620. The Shrovetide revels were particularly gay, and next day the Bishop of Winchester began Lent 'with an excellent sermon', and the crowds that had joined in the festivities thronged as readily to listen to Andrewes' words.

Yet all was not well at Whitehall, where Buckingham's jealous monopoly of power made life insecure for all he did not chance to favour. Foreign policy was particularly involved. King James was anxious to help his son-in-law whose brief tenure of the Bohemian crown had ended in disaster and whom the Spaniards were threatening to turn out of the Palatinate. James hoped to dissuade them by friendly overtures. He revived that grand design of marrying the heir to the English throne to a Spanish Infanta, which Prince Henry had refused to contemplate and which had been laid aside during the middle years, and he summoned a parliament in the hope of its support. But the Commons met in 1620 in no mood to sympathize with any Spanish alliance nor to supply the necessary money to proceed by more bellicose means. They were full of domestic grievances, from monopolies to religion. Andrewes preached the opening sermon stressing the King's power and authority and sent out James in quite the wrong mood to pacify them. To Andrewes, the patriarchal nature of the royal office meant that mercy and justice and righteousness must be the kingly attributes, but the Commons of England saw little of such qualities in a court where corruption was rampant, the Admiralty mismanaged by Buckingham, and bribery the rule in high offices of state. In 1621 their quarry was Bacon, who was proved to have taken bribes none the less readily that he did not let them affect his judgment. Andrewes was one of those commissioned to call on the discredited genius, to receive from him the great seal which was later given to Bishop Williams as Lord-Keeper. Bacon must surely have felt an unaccustomed turmoil of feelings as his old friend faced him. Of what Andrewes felt beyond a deep pity one cannot tell. Of the deep pity one can be certain.

One knows less than one would like of Andrewes as a bishop, but his deep sense of the divine authority with which bishops were invested imposed upon him the duty, conscientiously fulfilled, of being a worthy shepherd of his flock. Hacket, in describing Williams' life as Bishop of Lincoln, gives an illuminating account of the duties and delights of the episcopal office, describing in detail the Bishop's good management, the excellence of his chapel services (for Williams was a Welshman and a keen musician) and the hospitality he showed to all and sundry. Strangers passing by, the neighbouring clergy, 'the very yeomanry of fashion of the adjacent towns' were all alike welcome at Bishop Williams' table. 'The Poor were sharers in this Hospitality, in which serious discourse and Scripture reading accompanied the repast: and not only was there good fare for mind and body, there were also if need be, alms.' 'Except Bishop Andrewes,' Hacket commented, 'who was sublime in all vertue, there was not so great a Giver of his Order [as Bishop Williams] to the

supply of the Learned, and of Gentlemen of hard Fortune.'
It was these same qualities of hospitality and generosity which
had a high place in the attributes which Buckeridge ascribed
to Andrewes in his funeral sermon, while Aubrey made special
mention of Andrewes' concern to find out good men in the
diocese who were 'staked to poor livings' and to offer them
preferment. He had his own way of doing this, as in the
case of one Nicholas Fuller of whom Aubrey writes: 'The
Bishop sent for him and the poor man was afraid and knew
not what hurt he had done. . . . [He] made him sit down to
dinner and after the dessert, was brought in in a dish his
institution and induction or the donation of a prebend.' Those
who petitioned for rich livings, on the other hand, seldom
received a favourable reply.

It was by their triennial visitations that the bishops exerted
episcopal vigilance over their whole see. The first of the
articles to be enquired of by the church wardens and 'Sworne-
men' in Andrewes' first visitation of Winchester diocese in
1619 dealt with the church building itself, whether it was
'well and sufficiently repaired, the windows well glazed, the
floors plain and even, without dust, or anything noisome or
unseemly'. This was according to the accustomed form as
were the majority of the later articles, which, none the less,
give a fair picture of the ordered seemliness both in life and
worship which it was the aim of men like Andrewes and Overall, Laud and Sanderson to inculcate into their flocks. The
proper furnishing of the church, the seats cleanly kept 'and
the Parishoners in them . . . orderly set' with no 'contention or striving for any seat or place amongst them' was to be
a fit setting for the regular and devout administration of the
Sacrament. Not only notorious sinners, but any who had
openly and maliciously contended with his neighbour, ought
to be excluded, but Andrewes, anxious as always to save rather
than to censure, made special enquiry 'whether doth your
Minister before the several times of the administration of the
Lord's supper admonish and exhort his parishoners, if they
have their consciences troubled and disquieted, to resort unto

him or some other learned minister and open his grief that
he may receive such ghostly counsel and comfort as his conscience may be relieved and by the minister he may receive the
benefit of absolution '.

In each visitation there were various questions about the
schooling provided, particularly for the children of recusants
and separatists, and about the learning and character of the
priest. Andrewes was particularly anxious to lessen if he could
the evils of non-residence and the other abuses, so patent in
1604 and not yet eradicated. Had the minister, the church
wardens were asked, been ' admitted into Holy Orders by any
corrupt means of gift or promise. Or came he to his Benefice
by any compact for money, or for releasing the Patron's or
any other tithes. . . . When he is absent hath he an allowed
Preacher for his Curate. . . . What is his Curate's name and
how long hath he been Curate? And who was Curate before
and what is become of him. . . ? ' There was no aspect of
life or governance in every parish in his diocese that Andrewes
did not regard as his concern: certainly he wished to know of
any ' who came late to church or gave themselves to walk or
babble while the service was in progress '. In his final visitation, when the disputes that were to embitter Charles' reign
were becoming more evident, there were specific enquiries as
to the presence of a rood-screen. ' If not, when and by whom
and by what authority was it taken down? ' And as to the
right use of the Communion Table, had it been ' abused by
sitting on it, throwing hats on it, writing on it, or otherwise,
as is not agreeable to the holy use of it '. And finally Bishop
Andrewes was concerned to know that none had spoken
against His Majesty's supremacy and that the minister had
used ' the prayer for Christ's Catholic Church '.

In 1621 a tragic incident occurred. Archbishop Abbot,
' invited to some hunting sports ' and ' pretending to be a
wood-man took a cross-bow to make a shot at a Buck '. A
keeper was beating up the herd and the Archbishop let fly too
soon; ' his arrow meeting with a small bough in the way, was
cast a little from the mark, and by an unhappy glance wounded

the keeper in the arm. It was but a flesh wound and a slight one; yet being under the care of a heedless surgeon, the Fellow died of it next day.'

Here was a predicament 'which made work for Learned men to turn over their books'. The Primate of All England was guilty of manslaughter. The secular penalties could be remitted, but a grave problem remained. How could the Archbishop, his person tainted with blood, consecrate bishops, ordain priests or administer the sacraments? Neither Williams, recently appointed to the see of Lincoln, nor Laud, bishop-elect of St. David's, would agree to be consecrated by Abbot, Williams commenting: 'To leave a Man of blood Primate and Patriarch of all his churches is a thing that sounds very harsh in the old Councils and Canons of the Church.' There was a strong feeling that he ought to retire and spend the rest of his days in fasting and prayer.

Such a state of indecision could not continue. James wisely appointed a commission composed of six bishops and four laymen, to whom certain specific questions were submitted: whether the position of the Archbishop was irregular, whether this tended to a scandal, and how he could be restored? On the first and crucial question of irregularity, all of the bishops except Andrewes declared against Abbot, but Andrewes, as so often before, put common sense and charity before rule and precedent. He reminded his brethren that all might be in a like case and pleaded with them not to be too strict. His vigorous words swayed the balance in Abbot's favour, and he again advised the King to take immediate action that the whole unfortunate incident might be closed. James thereupon issued a full pardon under the great seal, and, until his death in 1632, Abbott remained Archbishop. He never recovered from the shock of the unhappy affair, and he did not forget that it was Andrewes, whom he had regarded as a rival, who had spoken out in his favour and proved himself true friend.

The reign was drawing to its close. Andrewes preached the Gowrie sermon at Windsor in August 1622 but he was exhausted afterwards, as Chamberlain reported. 'His voice grows very low but otherwise he did extraordinarily well and like himself. I dined with him that day and could not leave him till half an hour after six o'clock. The weather was very hot and he so faint and wet that he was fair to go to bed for some little time after he came out of the pulpit.' Like his royal master the Bishop was nearing the end. It was not a happy time for, early in 1623, Buckingham had conceived the mad idea of visiting Madrid so that Charles could do his courting for himself. The King had been cajoled into consenting and 'Steenie' and Baby Charles slipped out of England incognito. At first they were enthusiastic about their reception in Spain, and the marriage articles were actually drawn up and solemnly sworn to by King James, in Andrewes' presence, one of the last public ceremonies in which the latter took part. But away in Madrid, Buckingham's temper altered as his own excesses in speech and behaviour alienated his punctilious hosts, and even Prince Charles grew tired of courting a Princess he never saw. They returned to England in October, as precipitately as they left it, and an additional clause was inserted in the articles demanding the restoration of the Palatinate which, in effect, put an end to the unhappy project.

Andrewes was now an invalid at Winchester House and thither he summoned Matthew Wren, the Prince's chaplain, who had been with Charles in Madrid. Wren, on arrival, found Laud, the Bishop of St. David's, and Neile (now Bishop of Durham) closeted with Andrewes. The latter as was his custom kept silent while the others anxiously interrogated Wren: 'how the Prince's heart stands to the Church of England, that when God brings him to the Crown we may know what to hope for.' Wren did not hesitate to answer that he had even more confidence in Charles than in King James, despite the latter's greater learning. For a while they went on talking, and then Andrewes spoke, terminating the interview by the very gravity of his words. Turning to Wren, he said, kindly, 'Well doctor, God send you may be a true prophet concerning your Master's inclinations in those particulars, which we are glad to hear from you.' Then he added: 'I am sure I shall be a true prophet. I shall be in my grave, and so shall you, my lord of Durham. But my lord of St. David's and you, doctor, will live to see that day that your master will be put to it upon his head and his crown, without he will forsake the support of his Church.' In one detail only did the prophet err; four years before King Charles faced the supreme test and died in the faith he had consistently championed, William Laud, his mentor in all things spiritual, had gone to the block on Tower Hill, an old and broken man.

After a bitter year in which, impelled by his son and his favourite, he found himself, the Peace-maker, at war with Spain and met yet another Parliament, that even now failed to be satisfied, King James died in the spring of 1625, calling in his last hours for the Bishop whose words had never failed to delight and sustain him. But Andrewes could not come. He too lay on a bed of sickness and bitter indeed must have been the knowledge that at the end he could not answer the cry of the master he had served so faithfully. Andrewes recovered on this occasion but he knew his own passing would not be long delayed. He turned to setting his affairs in order, and in the pages of his will the personality of Lancelot Andrewes emerges very clearly. Here is the man, practical, imaginative, kind, whom it has sometimes been hard to find beneath the Bishop's vestments or the Privy-Councillor's gown. The tangled skein of political intrigue, his own dark forebodings as to the future that the young King must face, no longer lay heavy on his heart as he turned his thoughts to the brothers and sisters who had grown up with him in Barking and to the misfits of life whose succour was, all day and every day, his deep concern.

He thought first of his own passing and desired that at his funeral he should be attended by seventy or more old men, according to the number of his years. It was not, he thought, sufficient for them to have new gowns; he wanted them to be well and truly clad, that they at least to the end of their days should never shiver in rags; cassock and jerkin, shoes and hats, he listed the articles with pleasure and thoroughness.

And his mind ranging back over the London he knew and loved, he laid down that they should be chosen from the parishes where he had dwelt: All Hallows by the Tower, where he was christened, and St. Giles within Cripplegate where, as a young man, he had urged humility upon the rich, obedience upon the poor, and good works, the fruits of repentance, upon all. There were also St. Martin's within Ludgate, St. Andrewes' in Holborn and St. Saviour's Southwark, where the town houses of his bishoprics were situate, and from these five, the poor men were to come, though in his usual careful way the Bishop adds: 'Yet not excepting any that shall have more neede.'

His thoughts turned then to his College, where for fifteen years he had lived in true contentment of spirit. He could wish no man anything better, and he set aside £2,000 to provide for two Fellowships at Pembroke, to be held if possible by men who had come up as scholars of Dr. Watts' foundation. So he linked his own name with that of the man through whose help he had first come to Cambridge where he had been so much more truly at home than at Whitehall or Winchester House.

Next he set aside legacies for numerous nephews and nieces, in sums of ten and twenty pounds, increasing these amounts in a later codicil when he discovered his fortune was larger than he had ever realized. There was also a bequest to the son of his old headmaster, for Andrewes had never forgotten Dr. Mulcaster, whose portrait had always hung above the fireplace in his study.

He next allotted £2,000 to purchase land, which should produce an annual income of £100 divided into four equal portions. On Midsummer Eve, £25 was to go to seven aged and impotent persons, special regard being had to those who in earlier days 'did truly labour for their living'. At Michaelmas £25 went to seven 'poore fatherless children', in which number noted Andrewes, 'I comprehend such as goe up and down the streets from doore to doore, begging'. On January 3rd there was to be a distribution to 'aged widdowes' of fifty years or over 'each of whom had been wife to one husband only and were of honest conversation and report'. In Holy Week, the final £25 was to be distributed to seven prisoners, preferably from Southwark. Later Andrewes allotted a further sum for the relief of old and impotent mariners. That completed the will, except for the gift of gold rings to certain of his friends, in particular his fellow bishops. Sir Thomas and Lady Lake were among those he thus remembered, and there was also a gift for their son Lancelot, his godson. Lady Lake's reputation in history is that of a shrew; let it stand to her credit that she was Andrewes' friend.

It only remained to die. Death, for Andrewes, was no easy thing. He was too conscious of God's immaculate goodness to take lightly the summons to cross into the unknown where he did not for a moment doubt he must give an account of his stewardship. Yet deeper than a natural dread of judgment was the abiding faith in the power of the risen Christ to redeem and comfort and sustain. Neither death nor life, the weariness of old age nor the errors of maturity, the shrinking from pain of a naturally timid temperament, the consciousness of things amiss, and of a challenge threatening the very structure of the Church it had been his life work to maintain: none of these things could separate him from the love of God which was in Christ Jesus his Lord. During the last twelve months of his life he grew increasingly infirm, and in December 1625 was laid up for many weeks with the ague, the stone and the gout all at once. One of his brothers died in that year's epidemic and another shortly afterwards and Andrewes was much affected by their deaths. But he had recovered sufficiently in the new year to attend King Charles' coronation, and to preside at Winchester House over an episcopal commission of enquiry into the writings of Richard Montague, the High Church clergyman whose tracts had been denounced in Charles' first Parliament. Montague was vindicated but the Commission required the King to 'prohibit all parties, members of the Church of England, any further controversy of these questions by public preaching or writing or any other way, to the disturbance of the peace of the Church for the time to come'. It was Andrewes' voice speaking, Andrewes about to die, reiterating the faith of his lifetime that what was necessary to salvation God had made plain, that disputes and controversies meant an intrusion of self and so an intrusion of sin into the contemplation of divine grace; and that man's need—and his own—was not to debate but to pray— pray—pray. In prayer, and in prayer alone, the last months of his life were passed, while his pacific counsels were translated by more didactic tempers into something approaching defiance of parliamentary criticism. Through the windows of Winchester Palace the sounds and smells of the busy riverside traffic must have reached the old man as he bent at prayer in his closet or lay in pain on his sick-bed. The intercessions, so wide in their sympathy, so human in their understanding, that take up many pages of the book of private prayers, prove that he who never kept himself aloof from his fellows, was mindful of them still. But as the August heats, the stench of the wharves and the fear of pestilence gave way to the fresh breezes and the golden serenity of autumn, Bishop Andrewes put the world aside and early on the morning of September 25th, praying to the end, he died.

X

THE DEVOTIONS

THE STORY is told and the books of reference are back upon their shelves. In the Cathedral Church of Southwark lies the tomb of Lancelot Andrewes, below the vaulted roof of a chancel that is one of the loveliest in England. There is a prayer desk beside the tomb, and on it a copy of those private devotions, which in the last years of failing health were never far from his reach, the original volume 'happy in the glorious deformity thereof, being slubbered with his pious hands and watered with his pentential tears'.

As one kneels beside the tomb, turning the pages of the *Preces Privatae,* the life of the church of to-day goes on about one. It may be that a midday service is in progress, the congregation largely composed of business men and women. From without come the sounds of the Borough market, and every few moments a train thunders overhead, as if indeed all the hosts of Midian were about to assault the dwelling-place of the Most High. If the spirit of Lancelot Andrewes could return to life to-day, what point of contact would he find with this crowded, tortured civilization of the mid-twentieth century, with these men and women stealing away for half an hour from the busy round of wage-earning as he once was wont to leave Whitehall for the solace of his closet? Where once stood Winchester House is now a huddle of wharves and mean streets; the created world he loved to ponder is marred, it seems, beyond repair; and the problems that beset those who kneel in prayer are more complex, and as shadowed with fear and insecurity as any that troubled those who walked in Paul's when Andrewes sought to aid them. How can prayer of his help the men and women of to-day?

As if in answer, the words of the collect sound through the shadowed aisles: 'O God, who knowest us to be set in the midst of so many and great dangers that by reason of the frailty of our nature we cannot always stand upright. . . .'; or '. . . keep us, we beseech thee, from all things that may hurt us, that we being ready both in body and soul may cheerfully accomplish those things that thou wouldst have done'. Whatever the season, Epiphany or Easter or Trinity, the words strike home with their continued relevance and power.

These collects, the accredited mintage of the Church in prayer, are the prayers that Lancelot Andrewes used. They summed up for his generation as for ours the basic needs, the indefinable yearnings of mankind for guidance, enlightenment, strength of will and the grace of God in one's heart. If, indeed, Christian living is a steady pilgrimage in well-doing, with constant set-backs, renewed repentance and a deepening sense of fellowship, then the collects are milestones along the road, comforting and upholding through the centuries those who pray to the Almighty God who knows 'our necessities before we ask and our ignorance in asking'.

The *Preces Privatae* remain relevant just because they are not Andrewes' original compositions but a glorious bejewelled patchwork of liturgical worship drawn out of the reserves of learning he had accumulated since his boyhood, culled from the Eastern Church, from the Early Fathers, above all from the Bible and the Prayer Book and the psalms, that sublime handbook of praise and thanksgiving. These diverse mosaics have been set into a pattern by one who knew prayer to be a costly matter and who gave to its practice the devotion of his whole being. For worship to him, whether in the ordered beauty of the cathedral or in the privacy of the closet, demanded the whole being. 'It is true,' he wrote, 'that the life of prayer and thanksgiving standeth herein that we sing

praises with understanding, that we do *orare mente et spiritu.*'
'Herein stands the soul of prayer but as we ourselves have not
only a soul but a body also, so our prayer must have a body,
our tongue must be the pen of a ready writer', and vocal
prayer had a place in man's devotions as the body upon which
the soul could raise its petitions and its praise. He gave
clear directions also as to how and when to pray, for he
never believed in leaving such matters to the unreliable
promptings of personal desire and inspiration. One prayed of
necessity, in time of tribulation or penitence, but prayer
remained at all times 'our bounden duty and service' only
to be properly rendered if fixed hours were set aside for the
purpose. 'We are to learn so to settle ourselves to prayer,' he
added, 'as that nothing should cause us to break off, and so to
regard others that are occupied in this duty as by no means
to interrupt them.' He proceeded then to outline the com-
ponent parts of prayer; the garment of praise in which all true
devotion must be clad, and the penitence that to be effective
must be specific, to which end he advised a nightly self-
examination. 'The heart is deceitful above all things; the
heart is deep and full of windings; the old man is covered in
a thousand wrappings.' The self-abasement of the Bishop's
deprecations and the exaggeration of much of the language
in the portion of the *Preces* devoted to penitence is alien to our
time and spirit, but the deep humility that engendered it is the
mark of a saint, coming as it did not merely from the lips but
from the heart.

There is more of thanksgiving than petition in Andrewes'
prayers, but on this matter of asking things of God he had
much to say in his sermons. His starting point was the
gospel: 'Ask and it shall be given unto you, seek and ye
shall find, knock and the door will be open.' 'Ask in confidence and trust, seek with diligence; knock and persevere.'
For, as was natural in one who had worked hard all his life,
Andrewes argued that those who ask must also seek. 'He
that having prayed, still without adding his endeavour shall
not receive the thing he prays for, for he must not only *orare*

but *laborare*. . . .' Moreover he must endeavour to ask with
wisdom as well as diligence. 'As he is our physician, He will
not give us cold drink when we are sick of an ague though
we cry for it never so much. They that ask vengeance of God
and would have Him to be the executioner of their wrath shall
not be heard . . . but God our heavenly Father as He know-
eth best what is good for us so He will give us good things,
tho' we be not able always to ask that which is good for ourselves.'

But it is in his intercessions that Andrewes' nature shines
most clearly through the *Preces Privatae* for as he prayed for
'all sorts and conditions of men', listing their needs and his
hopes for their welfare in the same meticulous way in which
he listed the benefits for which he had cause to be thankful,
all the tenderness and large-heartedness of the man spilt over
in anxious and loving prayer not only for those for whom he
was in duty bound to pray, but for all upon whom his kindly
glance had lingered in the London streets or the country lanes
of his diocese, 'for the succour and consolation of all with
whom it fareth ill in mind or body', for women labouring
with child, for captives and wayfarers, for the rising generation and for those 'in any sort in jeopardy especially them
that pray not'.

All true prayer, Andrewes asserted, must begin with the
double premise: 'We are not able of ourselves to think any
good of ourselves', and 'our sufficiency is of God'. It is
indeed well for us that the Holy Spirit 'doth help our infirmities', those infirmities which are the same in every age.
Andrewes knew as well as any the cold heart, the faltering
words, the wandering thoughts and wanton images that work
havoc with the half-done prayer. Only God's Spirit sufficeth
to draw us back to Himself, to give us of a sudden the desire
to pray. And if our own hearts remain cold, 'there are of
God's saints that pray for us with all instancy', as Andrewes
was careful to remind his hearers, for 'the faithful, howsoever
they be many and dispersed into divers corners of the world
yet they are but one body and as they are members of one

body, so they pray not privately for themselves but for the whole body of the Church, so that the weakness of one member is supplied by the fervent and earnest prayer of the other '. It was in this belief that Andrewes prayed as one to whom the communion of saints was a living reality.

The original volume of the *Preces Privatae*, which Richard Drake described in 1648 as marked by Andrewes' tears and soiled by constant use, has probably not been preserved. There is, however, in existence, recovered from a dealer in 1883, the copy given by Andrewes himself to Laud, shortly before the latter became Bishop of Bath and Wells. Some have claimed this to be the original, but it was more probably made by an amanuensis, for apart from dissimilarities in the handwriting of the Greek portions, the Hebrew text is too incorrect for it to have been made by Andrewes himself. A second copy, now housed appropriately in Pembroke College, Cambridge, was made by Samuel Wright who had been one of Andrewes' secretaries and later registrar to Matthew Wren, the then Bishop of Ely. Wright was a great friend of Dr. Drake's, the Fellow of Pembroke who first published the prayers, and gave him the copy he had made. Originally the manuscript had many omissions, some of which have been supplied by Drake and by later commentators. There is also a manuscript in Latin in the Harleian MSS in the British Museum, and this contains devotions, differing from those in the Greek MS but certainly by Andrewes. At the time of the Tractarian revival, the Greek text was translated by Newman with a grace and brilliance which gave to the prayers something of his own rare spirit, and the work was completed by Neale's version of the Latin *Preces*. Among later scholars who have translated the prayers are the great Presbyterian Divine, Alexander Whyte, who prefaced his edition with an interesting life of Andrewes, and R. E. Brightman of Oxford whose text and notes and analytical introduction are alike full of sound learning and of sympathetic understanding of Andrewes' churchmanship.

The *Preces Privatae* consist of a number of acts of worship for regular or occasional use, and begin with a series of daily prayers, a different form for every morning of the week and three slightly different versions of evening prayer. The morning devotions follow the same order every day; an opening sentence introduces an act of commemoration and worship, and then come confession and penitence, ending with a prayer for grace. This is followed each day by an act of Faith, based usually on the Creed, and a brief act of Hope as Andrewes turns from his contemplation of the eternal verities to the needs of the whole world. After the intercessions, come the blessing and commendations, and at the end are the particular thanksgivings and a triumphant act of Praise. Each day a different stress has been laid on the various aspects of prayer: on Wednesday, for example, the intercessions are prominent; whereas on Friday there are lengthy thanksgivings. In some cases the terse notes are little more than guides to meditation; at others the flowing liturgical phrases have a lyrical beauty, strong and tender in tone. Andrewes' consciousness of words and their exact meaning never left him even in his prayers and perhaps in consequence they lack something of mystical depth and beauty, but they came from the heart of one who understood more than most the richness and universality of God's love. One should note also the personal attention that has gone to their compilation. Andrewes was never content with a vague assertion of thankfulness, he was grateful not only for the gifts of the spirit and the beauty of the world about him, but for every specific memory of parents, of school masters and friends, for honours gained and opportunities of service, for all that had conditioned him and made him what he was. But it is significant that these particular thanksgivings, and indeed the whole prayer, is set against the background of the Creation. It was not for nothing that all his life Andrewes had been intensely interested in the natural world about him, seeing no disharmony between things spiritual and things material. The idea meant much to him of an ordered universe, revealing a Creator, whose rule was one of law and purpose, and his first impulse in worship every morning was to ponder the act of Creation which the day commemorated.

In the ensuing examples, some part of each section of the Sunday order of prayer has been included; on subsequent days, after the opening act of commemoration, the excerpts chosen have been such as seem best to illustrate the character of his devotion. Most of the lengthy acts of penitence have been omitted, but their existence should be borne in mind. Every day the same sequence was usually followed; a contemplation of God's creative power; a self-abasement before His Majesty; an assertion of faith and hope in His redeeming love; intercession for the needs of the world, praise and thanksgiving, and glory to God in the Highest.

XI

COURSE OF PRAYERS
FOR THE WEEK[1]

The First Day

SUNDAY

Introduction:

Through the tender mercies of our God the
Day-Spring from on high hath visited us.

Glory be to Thee, O Lord, glory to Thee
    Creator of the light,
  and Enlightener of the world.
Thou who didst create the Visible light,
    The sun's rays, a flame of fire,
  day and night, evening and morning.
Thou who didst create the light invisible,
    The light which never sets,
  that which may be known of God,
  the Law written in the heart,
    Oracle of Prophets,
    melody of psalms,
    instruction of Proverbs,
    experience of Histories.

. . . .

Thou who didst send down on Thy disciples on this day
    Thy Thrice Holy Spirit,

[1] *The Private Devotions of Lancelot Andrewes*, edited by Edmund Venables
from J. H. Newman's translation and published by Suttaby & Co., London,
1883.

Withdraw not Thou the gift, O Lord, from us,
  but renew it in us, day by day,
    who ask Thee for it.

Confession
    Merciful and pitiful Lord,
    Long-suffering and of great mercy,
I have sinned, Lord, I have sinned against Thee.

      . . . . . .

    I conceal nothing,
    I make not excuses . . .
For me, I forget not my sins,
    they are ever before me,
I remember them in the bitterness of my soul.

      . . . . . .

    I repent, O Lord, I repent,
    Lord, help Thou mine impenitence
      And more and still more
    pierce Thou, rend, crush my heart
    and remit, forgive, pardon
what things are grief to me, and offence of heart.

      . . . . . .

    and in due time, Lord, say to me
Be of good cheer, thy sins are forgiven thee,
    My grace is sufficient for thee.

Prayer for Grace . . .
    Open Thou mine eyes that I may see,
    incline my heart that I may desire
    order my steps that I may follow
    the way of Thy commandments.
    . . . .

Preparation for Public worship . . .
Remember, O Lord, our brethren that are
    around us,

And praying with us at this holy hour
   for their zeal and earnestness' sake,
Remember also those who on reasonable
   causes are absent,
And have mercy on them and on us
   according to the multitude of Thy mercies.

Profession
   I believe, O Lord, in Thee
   Father, Word, Spirit, One God.
That by the fatherly love and power
   all things were created;
That by Thy goodness and love to man
All things have been gathered together
   in one in Thy Word
Who for us men and for our salvation
   was made flesh . . .
   This most holy faith
   which was once delivered to the Saints
I believe, O Lord; help Thou mine unbelief.

Intercession
O Thou that art the Hope of all the ends of the earth,
remember Thy whole creation for good, visit the
   world in Thy compassion . . .
O Thou that walkest in the midst of the golden candlesticks
remove not our candlestick out of its place,
Set in order the things that are wanting,
   Strengthen the things that remain.
       .   .   .   .   .

   O Thou by Whom are ordained the powers that be
   Grant to those who are chief at Court,
      to be chief in virtue and Thy fear;
   Grant to the Parliament Thy holy wisdom;
   To those in power, to have no power against the truth
      but for the truth. . . .
       .   .   .   .   .

Grant to Farmers and Keepers of cattle good seasons;
To the Fleet and fishers fair weather;
To tradesmen, not to overreach one another;
To Mechanics, to pursue their business lawfully,
  even to the meanest workmen,
  even down to the Poor. . . .
Do Thou arise and have mercy
  on those who are in the last necessity.
  . . . .

All in extreme age and weakness
All tempted to suicide
All troubled by unclean spirits,
the despairing, the sick in soul or body,
  the faint-hearted.
All in prison and chains, all under sentence of death,
orphans, widows, foreigners, travellers, voyagers,
women with child, women who give suck,
All in bitter servitude, or in the mines, or in the galleys,
Or in loneliness.

  .   .   .   .   .   .

O Lord I commend to Thee,
  my soul and my body,
  my mind and my thoughts,
  my prayers, and my vows,
  my senses and my limbs,
  my words and my works,
  my life and my death;
my brothers and my sisters, and their children,
my friends, my benefactors, my well-wishers,
  those who have a claim on me;
  my kindred and my neighbours,
  my country and all christendom.

Praise
  Up with our hearts;
  we lift them up unto the Lord

As it is meet, and right, and fitting and due,
  in all things and for all things.
At all times, in all places, by all means
  in every season, every spot,
  ever, everywhere, everyway
To make mention of Thee, to worship Thee . . .
  to give thanks to Thee
Who art the Maker, Nourisher, Preserver,
  Governor,
Protector, Author, Finisher of all . . .

The Second Day

MONDAY
  My voice shalt Thou hear betimes, O Lord;
    early in the morning
  will I direct my prayer unto Thee
    And Thou wilt look upon me.
      Blessed art Thou, O Lord
  Who didst create the firmament of heaven . . .
  The waters above the heavens, mists and
    exhalations,
  for showers, dew, hail, snow as wool
    hoar frost as ashes, ice as morsels,
    clouds from the ends of the earth,
  lightnings, thunders, winds out of Thy
    treasures, tempests;
  Waters beneath the heavens,
  for drinking and for bathing.

Prayer for Grace . . .
  Grant to me
    1. to be religious and pious
    2. to worship and serve
    3. to bless faithfully and to swear truly
    4. to confess meetly in the congregation

5. affection and obedience,
6. patience and good temper,
7. purity and soberness
8. contentedness and goodness
9. truth and incorruptness
10. good thoughts, perseverance to the end.

Intercession
Let us beseech God, on behalf of the whole creation . . .

For the succour and comfort of all who are dispirited,
  infirm, in want, unsettled,
  both men and women.
For thankfulness and sobriety in all
  who are cheerful, healthy, prosperous, quiet, both men and
  women,
For the Catholic Church,
  its establishment and increase;
For the Eastern,
  its deliverance and union,
for the Western,
  its renovation and peace;
for the British,
  the supply of what is wanting in it,
  the strengthening of what remains in it.
  . . . .
for the rising generation . . .
for those who have a claim on me
  from relationship . . .
  or from benefits conferred . . .
Or from trust placed in me,
  for all whom I have educated,
  all whom I have ordained;
  for my College, my Parish
  Southwell, St. Paul's Westminster,
  dioceses of Chichester, Ely and my present.
  . . . .

Or from natural kindness,
    for all who love me, though some of them I know not;
Or from Christian love,
    for those who hate me without cause, . . .
Or from neighbourhood,
    for all who dwell near me peaceably and harmlessly,
. . . .

Or from stress of engagements,
    For all who for reasonable causes,
      fail to call upon Thee

     .   .   .   .

    For all who are undertaking any good work
    Which will bring glory to the Name of God
      or some great good to the Church;
       For all who act nobly
      either towards things sacred or towards
       the poor;
    For all who have ever been offended by me
      either in word or in deed.

God have mercy on me and bless me.

     .   .   .   .

    Renew me thoroughly, O God,
    for if Thou wilt, Thou canst.

The Third Day

TUESDAY
Introduction
    O God, Thou art my God,
      early will I seek Thee.
    Blessed art Thou, O Lord,
Who gatheredest the waters into the sea,
And broughtest to sight the earth,
And madest to sprout from it herb and fruit tree . . .
the green things for food, enjoyment, medicine . . .

And things beneath the earth,
Stone, metals, minerals, coal
blood and fire and vapours of smoke.

Praise . . .
My soul doth praise the Lord,
　for the goodness He hath done
　　to the whole Creation,
　and to the whole race of men,
　for Thy mercies towards myself . . .
　for all successes, now or heretofore
　　for any good thing done;
　for health, credit, competency, safety, gentle estate, quiet.

Thou has not cut off as a weaver my life,
　nor from morning even to night made an end of me.
　　　　.　　.　　.　　.　　.

Thou hast holden my soul in life,
And wilt not suffer my foot to slip . . .

The Fourth Day

WEDNESDAY
Introduction
　I have thought upon Thee, O Lord
　　when I was waking
　for Thou hast been my helper.

　Blessed art Thou, O Lord,
　who madest the two Lights, Sun and Moon,
　the greater and the lesser,
　　and the stars
　for light, for signs, for seasons . . .
　　to rule over day and night.
　　　.　　.　　.　　.　　.

Intercession

Remember . . .
Thy Holy Church from one end
of the earth to the other, and give
her peace.

.   .   .   .   .   .

Remember every Christian soul,
in affliction, in distress and in trial.

.   .   .   .   .   .

Remember religious and faithful kings;
and especially remember, Lord, our
divinely-guarded king.
Vouchsafe to him deep and undisturbed peace,
that in his serenity
We may lead a quiet and peaceable life
with all godliness and honesty.

.   .   .   .   .   .

Fill our garners with all manner of store,
Preserve our marriages in peace and concord
nourish our infants,
guide our youth,
sustain our aged,
comfort the weak-hearted,
gather together the scattered,
bring back the wanderers,
and knit them to Thy Holy Catholic Apostolic Church
. . . .

O Thou who knowest each man and his petition,
each house and its need,
deliver, O Lord this city,
And all the country in which we sojourn,
from plague, famine, earthquake, flood,
fire, sword, hostile invasion and civil war.
End the schisms of the Churches,
Still the ragings of the Heathen,
And receive us all into Thy kingdom,
Acknowledging us as children of light,

And Thy peace and love
vouchsafe to us, O Lord our God.

· · · · · ·

Be Lord,
within me to strengthen me,
without me to guard me,
above me to shelter me,
beneath me to uphold me,
before me to direct me,
after me to bring me back,
round about me to secure me.

The Fifth Day

THURSDAY
Introduction
May we be satisfied with Thy
    mercy, O Lord, in the morning.

Blessed art Thou, O Lord
Who broughtest forth from the water,
creeping things that have life,
and whales, and winged fowl.

Be Thou exalted, O God, above the heavens
    and Thy glory above all the earth.
By Thy Ascension, O Lord,
    draw us too after Thee,
that we may set our minds on
    what is above,
not on things on the earth.

Prayer for Grace
Give me grace
    To lay aside every weight,
And the sin which doth so easily beset me . . .

Give me grace to be poor in spirit,
  to mourn that I may be comforted,
  to be meek that I may inherit the earth,
  to hunger and thirst after righteousness,
    that I may be filled,
  to be pitiful that I may be pitied
  to be pure in heart, that I may see God . . .

Profession
  I, coming to God, believe that He is,
  and that He is a rewarder of them that
    diligently seek him.

  I know that my Redeemer liveth
  that He is Christ, the Son of the Living God.
          .   .   .   .   .   .

  I believe to see the goodness of the Lord
    in the land of the living.

The Sixth Day

FRIDAY
Early shall my prayer come before Thee
  Blessed art Thou, O Lord,
  Who didst bring forth of the earth
  Wild beasts, cattle
  and all creeping things
  for food, clothing, help
And didst make man after Thy image
to rule the earth, and blessedst him.
          .   .   .   .   .   .

Blessed art Thou, O Lord,
For the holy Passion of this day
O by Thy sufferings on this day
for our salvation, save us, O Lord.

Confession

Lord remember me
when Thou comest in Thy kingdom,
Lord, lay not mine enemies' sins to their charge,
Lord, lay not my own to mine.

By Thy sweat, bloody and clotted,
Thy soul in agony,
Thy Head crowned with thorns,
bruised with staves
Thine Eyes wet with tears
Thine ears full of insults
Thy mouth moistened with vinegar and gall
. . . .

Thy Hands and Feet stabbed through
Thy strong cry, Eli, Eli
Thy Heart pierced with the spear
the Water and Blood thence flowing
Thy Body broken
Thy Blood poured out
Lord forgive the offence of Thy servant,
and cover all his sins.

Prayer for Grace

Help me to crucify the flesh and its works . . .
Help me to bring forth the fruits of the
Spirit . . .

Profession

I believe that Thou didst create me,
despise not the work of Thine own hands;
that Thou madest me after Thine own
image and likeness,
Suffer not Thy likeness to be blotted out . . .
that Thou didst redeem me with Thy Blood,
Suffer not the cost of that redemption
to perish.

.   .   .   .   .   .

That Thou didst graft me into the
    good olive tree:
The member of a mystical body, cut not off.

The Seventh Day

SATURDAY

O Lord be gracious unto us; we have waited for Thee,
be Thou our arm every morning, our salvation also in time
of trouble.

Blessed art Thou O Lord, who restedst on the seventh day
from all Thy works and blessedst and sanctifiedst it . . .

Prayer for Grace
    The power of the Father guide me;
    the wisdom of the Son enlighten me;
    the operation of the Spirit quicken me.

Guard Thou my soul, stablish my body, elevate my senses,
direct my converse, form my habits, bless my actions, fulfil
my prayers, inspire my holy thoughts, pardon the past, correct
the present, prevent the future. . . .

Now unto Him that is able to do exceeding, abundantly,
above all that we ask or think, according to the power that
worketh in us, to Him be glory in the Church, in Christ
unto all generations, world without end.

AMEN

INDEX